the Unofficial Guide® to Marketing Your Small Business

Marcia Layton Turner

WILEY

Wiley Publishing, Inc.

Contents

About the Author

Marcia Layton Turner is a former marketing consultant and business journalist who writes regularly about small business. Many of the books and articles she has penned have dealt with the challenge of generating revenue through more effective marketing techniques, but this is the first to pull all that information into one place.

Her previous titles include *The Unofficial Guide to Starting a Small Business, How to Think Like the World's Greatest Marketing Minds,* and *The Complete Idiot's Guide to Starting Your Own Business,* which she co-authored. Her work has also appeared in *Entrepreneur's StartUps, BusinessWeek, Business 2.0, Black Enterprise,* and *Woman's Day,* among many others.

Before striking out on her own, Marcia worked in marketing communications at Eastman Kodak Company. She earned her MBA from the University of Michigan and BA from Wellesley College.

Acknowledgements

Many people helped in the preparation of this book, offering ideas, suggestions, and examples that will certainly benefit the reader.

Thanks to Pam Mourouzis and Roxanne Cerda, two terrific Wiley acquisitions editors, for helping to make this book a reality.

I was thrilled when marketing guru Kimberly McCall agreed to serve as technical editor of the book. Her input and suggestions helped make it much stronger.

And I couldn't have asked for a better developmental editor in Tere Stouffer. She was supportive, encouraging, and creative, and certainly a key asset on the project.

Finally, to the small business owners who were willing to share their success stories and offer tips to other business owners, I sincerely appreciate your wisdom.

When it comes right down to it, successful businesses have an abundance of customers. Large or small, companies that are doing well have more customers than they can handle— which means they are easily able to cover their costs, reinvest in the company, and expand. Unfortunately, many small businesses struggle to reach this level of success, to find an admiring target market, and to develop business relationships with enough customers to stay in business. They struggle because they aren't using all the marketing tools they can; that is, their marketing is weak. Fortunately, there is a lot that can be done to turn the situation around or to get a small business started on the right foot.

The success linchpin

Success in business is predicated on a strong marketing program. And the good news for you is that this book is going to familiarize you with marketing techniques (some of which you may have never heard of), recommend the best ways to use them, and show you how best to spend your marketing budget, no matter how big or small it may be.

Marketing is about persuading potential customers to do business with you, by creating a brand image that reflects the kind of company you are and the kinds of products and services you sell, communicating all

xi

the reasons customers should choose to do business with you instead of your competitors, and delivering all that you promised in the way of performance and service. When you do that—promise to solve your customers' problems—and then come through for them, you develop potentially life-long relationships that are worth hundreds or thousands of dollars in revenue over the next few years.

Marketing defined

Although this book gives you specific steps you can take to make your business more attractive to potential customers, through advertising or publicity or slick marketing materials, marketing is more than those tactics. It's really everything you do to make people aware of your company and entice them to consider doing business with you. That's what marketing, done well, does: It convinces customers to buy from you.

One component you don't hear enough about in marketing is consistency. Consistency refers to all aspects of your marketing presenting a positive image of your business. Repetition of a marketing message and look increases the odds of a sale with each appearance. And, in the same way, every inconsistency reduces your credibility and potential revenue. If people you have hired to handle telemarketing for you are friendly and knowledgeable, the marketing materials that are mailed out are polished and professional, and the money-back guarantee reassuring, you can still lose the sale if your business's appearance is run-down or shoddy or simply does not match the image your other tactics portrayed. The image you are working to present through all your marketing efforts needs to be consistent 100 percent of the time.

Marketing ≠ sales

Everything you do to convince someone to do business with you is marketing—the networking, the direct mail campaign, the advertising, the Web site, the customer service—everything. And after a customer makes that decision, the process shifts from marketing to sales. The *sale* is literally the part of the process where money changes hands. Then you shift back to marketing to maintain a relationship with the customer that leads to other sales.

Marketing is not the same as sales, but both are part of an important cycle in helping a business be successful.

Getting started

To have a successful small business, all you really need to do is find and keep profitable customers, selling a product or service they believe they need. But to start, focus mainly on identifying and winning customers using as many marketing techniques as you can. Then carefully monitor how well each method performs. Finally, drop the tactics that aren't working and replace them with new ones, or with more of your current methods that are working.

Marketing is more art than science because each business is different and each customer is different, so determining which marketing method is going to work best for each company is nearly impossible to predict. So you test, tweak, and try again until you find the method that customers respond to more frequently.

In many ways, the key to success is in delighting every customer with quality and service beyond their expectations. Marketing is where those expectations are defined. When that happens, success is just around the corner.

Special features of this book

Every book in the Unofficial Guide series offers the following four special sidebars that are devised to help you get things done cheaply, efficiently, and intelligently.

- **Money Saver:** Tips and shortcuts that help you save money
- **Watch Out!:** Cautions and warnings to help you avoid common pitfalls
- **Bright Idea:** Smart or innovative ways to do something; in many cases, the ideas listed here help you save time or hassle
- **Quote:** Anecdotes from real people who are willing to share their experiences and insights

We also recognize your need to have quick information at your fingertips, and have provided the following comprehensive sections at the back of the book:

- **Glossary:** Definitions of complicated terminology and jargon
- **Resource Directory:** Lists of relevant agencies, associations, institutions, Web sites, and so on
- **Further Reading:** Suggested titles that can help you get more in-depth information on related topics
- **Index**

Marketing Matters

Zeroing In on Your Customer

Chapter 1

Whether you're planning a new business or working to boost sales in an existing company, it's always smart to start marketing by looking at where you expect your sales to come from: your customers. If you have an existing business, it's much easier to look back at who has bought from you in the past, of course.

Yes, your product or service is important, but unless you have people willing to pay money for it, your business isn't viable. For your company to stay in business, you need customers—but not all customers are equal. In fact, there are good customers and there are bad customers, and bad customers cost you money.

Unfortunately, you can't often tell a good customer from a bad one just by looking at them. It takes research to discover which customers are the most profitable and to be able to weed out the unprofitable ones, but it can be done.

Studying your customers helps you determine which marketing methods will work best for your particular company. By studying your sales records, you'll be able to divide your customer base into market segments—groups of customers with similar buying habits or needs—and to create marketing campaigns to increase sales from these segments. Grouping customers together by factors such as how far they have to travel to get to your business, how much they spend each month with you, or how old they are helps you create a more effective marketing program. Instead of using a single message to reach all of your different types of customers, you'll be able to create marketing messages that speak to each of your market segments, and encourage them to buy. And that's what marketing is all about isn't it—making money.

Divide and conquer

There are several ways to divide your customers into different market segments, including using the following characteristics:

- **Geographic:** Use a location as the common element, whether that's a home address, business site, or proximity to a particular mall.

- **Use-based:** Use the frequency of usage of a product or service as the commonality, such as airline flights per year, trips to the supermarket, or subscription to a particular magazine.

- **Benefit-oriented:** Use a focus on the benefits received from using a product or service as the shared bond, such as a desire to lose weight or save money; that is, the reason behind the purchase.

- **Psychographic:** Use lifestyle and an individual's preference for certain activities as an important factor, such as environmentally conscious purchasing habits or political activism. To find out more about segmenting your customers this way, check out www.examstutor.com/business/resources/ studyroom/marketing/market_analysis/8_psychographic_ segmentation.php.

- **Demographic:** Use personal characteristics, such as age, education level, or household income to group individuals.

The more you know about your different types of buyers, the more targeted your marketing can be, and, thus, the higher your sales.

That's not to say that marketing to everyone the same way never works. It can, but undifferentiated marketing, as mass marketing is often called, is also generally more expensive. To market to everyone, you need to use a method that has broad reach, such as advertising in a national business magazine or securing a product placement on the top-rated television show.

Mass advertising can work, but it's also very expensive to do well, and few small businesses have an overflowing budget. Which is why dividing your entire customer base into individual segments often works better. You can choose the marketing method that works best for each group and reduce the amount of money you waste by reaching people who aren't in your target market.

Segmenting your customer base also enables you to prioritize your many market segments and focus your marketing attention on those with the highest sales potential. Or you can target them all simultaneously, but with different marketing messages. It's up to you, but you need to have information about your target market in order to do that.

How many customers make a successful business?

Before you start segmenting your current customer base—dividing it into smaller groups of like customers—take a step back and assess how large your potential market is. That is, if you sold to everyone in your target market—the group of customers you want to sell to—how many customers would you have? And is that number enough to sustain your business, long-term? The answer depends on how profitable your product or service is, and how high your expenses and income goals are.

Bright Idea

To determine how large a particular target market is, check out www.infousa.com. Find out how many people live in a certain Zip code, or the number of pediatricians nationwide, for example. InfoUsa can give you a sense of whether your customer base is big enough to support your business.

Understanding that more customers generally means more sales, some small business owners elect to claim everyone and their brother as potential customers. They assume that if their potential market is huge—astronomical, even—their sales, likewise, should be huge. But, in fact, thinking that everyone is your customer is dangerous and can be very costly.

Although it's possible that all humans could use your product or service, such as if you are a doctor or a supermarket, for example, the reality is that you can't afford to market to all humans everywhere. Trying to alert all 6.6 billion humans on the earth of your products and services would put you out of business quickly.

A smarter approach is to limit your marketing focus to the group of humans likely to do the most business with you. That is, don't try to do business with everyone, just those most likely to buy from you. They may be customers within a certain radius of your location, such as five miles, individuals in a certain demographic group, such as moms of new babies, or they may be owners of a certain brand of automobile or computer.

All potential customers are not worth your time and money, however. Just go after the most profitable ones.

Don't know who those are? Start by looking at who is currently buying from you.

Who are you currently selling to?

To determine who is currently buying from you and why, consider creating a customer profile to help identify your major market segments.

A customer profile is a snapshot of who your customers are, how to reach them, and why they buy from you. Asking questions of your customers to learn more about them and their buying habits can help you choose marketing tools that work better than what you're currently using, and then save you money by dropping marketing methods that are ineffective.

Because every business's customers are different, there is no standard customer profile I can give you to use, but I can provide a series of questions for you to choose from so you can create your own. Add questions to your customer profile that help you understand your customer more. Each answer should help you choose how to spend your marketing dollars by telling you more about how, why, or when your customer makes the decision to buy from you.

Don't waste your customers' time asking questions that won't impact your marketing decision-making. For example, if you own a local pet store, finding out whether a customer personally owns a pet, and what kind, is critical information that will help you improve your marketing message to that person. But if you own a medical transcription company, knowing that your customer owns a pet may be interesting, but it's not at all useful in encouraging them to do more business with you. Stick to questions that tell you more about their habits, preferences, and needs, so you can address them when you provide marketing information.

Questions that help you determine how to divide your customers into different market segments include information about when, why, and how they buy.

- **When:** Is there a particular event or time of year that triggers a need for your services?

- **Why:** Do you have a particular expertise that some companies don't have on-staff, or a knack for remembering your customers by name?

- **How:** Are your customers frequenting one of your locations more than another, or buying online more this year than last?

For a consumer-focused company (versus a business-focused venture), possible questions include the following:

How long does it take to get to our location?
__ 5 minutes __ 10 minutes __ 15 minutes __ 20 minutes
__ more than 20 minutes

How many people are involved in the decision to buy from us?
__1 __ 2 __ 3–5 __ more than 5

How long have you been a customer? __ less than 6 months
__ 6–12 months __ 13–24 months __ more than 2 years

How many times a year do you buy from us?
__ 1 __ 2–4 __ 5–8 __ 9–13 __ more than 13

Approximately how much do you spend, on average, at each visit or project? $_____

Is there any particular product or service you rely on us to provide? _____

Do you buy from us for yourself or for someone else?
__ myself __ someone else __ both

What is it about our company that you like most? _____

What do you like least about us? _____

What one thing could we do that would encourage you to do more business with us? _____

How did you initially hear about us? __ friend __ newspaper article __ ad __ Web site __ direct mail __ drove by __ other: _____

How do you typically travel to us? __ car __ bus __ cab __ train __ on foot __ other: _____

 Watch Out!

If you gather personal information from your customers, you owe it to them to keep it confidential and to clearly state your privacy policy up front so they know you won't sell, rent, or loan your customer list with their names on it. If you do, you risk losing many customers.

For business-to-business market segments, more appropriate questions could include the following:

In what city is your headquarters located? _____

How many other locations or branches are there
        statewide/nationwide/worldwide? _____

How many people do you employ?
        __ full-time __ part-time __ contract

What are your annual revenues? $_____

In what industry does your company operate? _____

In what year was the company founded? _____

What is your top-selling product/service? _____

To develop your own customer profile, consider what information would help you serve your customer base better; that is, what kind of information are you currently lacking? Then use that to create your own customer profile form to distribute to your current customer base.

Type up a form and ask customers to fill it out. Depending on your type of business, you may be able to hand it to them as they stand in line at the check-out, leave it on the table or in a waiting room, mail it to them and ask them to return it, or direct them to a Web site where the questionnaire is available. Explain that you're making an effort to provide better service to them, your customers, and that their answers to your questions will help you do that.

After you have the information, you'll want to look at the profiles in bulk, to get a sense of the commonalities among your customers. Are they all buying from you because of a sudden trend? Do they buy because you're one of the few companies open at a particular hour? Look for important reasons why, when, and how your customers are buying in order to understand how to attract more like them.

Bright Idea

To encourage customers to fill out your form, offer an incentive, such as a gift card for a free cup of coffee or a percentage off their next purchase from you. The more time and personal information you want from your customers, the larger the reward you should offer.

Understanding demographics

Learning more about your customers' purchasing habits and buying preferences is only part of the puzzle—you also need to learn more about the person making the decision. Information about a person's background—their demographic characteristics—also helps you understand what makes them tick.

Demographic questions include the following:

How old are you? ___ under 19 __ 19–25 __ 26–35 __ 36–45 __ 46–55 __ 56–65 __ 66–75 __ over 75

What is your approximate household income?
__ less than $25,000 __ $25,00–40,000 __ $41,000–55,000 __ $56,000–70,000 __ $71,000–85,000 __ more than $85,000

Do you live in a(n): __single-family home __ condo __ apartment __ student housing __ retirement community

What is your gender? __ female __ male

What is the highest level of education you have attained?
__ high school attendance __ high school diploma __ some college __ college degree __ graduate coursework __ graduate degree __ postgraduate work

Are you: __ employed full-time __ employed part-time __ self-employed __ unemployed __ student __ retiree __ stay-at-home caregiver

How many hours per week do you work outside the home?
__ under 21 __ 21–35 __ 36–40 __ 41–50 __ more than 50

Do you have children? __ no __ yes

If yes, what are their ages? __ under age 2 __ 2–4 __ 5–10
    __ 11–15 __ 16–17 __ over 18

What Zip code do you live in? _____

What is your ethnic background? __ African-American
    __ Native American __ Asian American __ Hispanic
    __Caucasian __ other: _____

Information you gather about the demographic characteristics of your current customers can help you make marketing decisions. You may decide to adjust your marketing message, such as including both Spanish and English promotions if you discover the majority of your customers are of Hispanic heritage. You may find that it makes sense to explore new advertising vehicles, such as a senior citizen newsletter, should you learn that your best customers often travel from a certain center. Or you may discover you need to make some changes to the way your business operates, perhaps staying open later at night to accommodate professionals who leave work later than most.

Taking the time to fully describe your customer base—in terms of their relationship to your business (how they feel about it, how loyal they are, how often they buy, and so on) and their personal characteristics—can help you define categories of customers. From there, you can see how well those existing customers match your definition of the perfect customer.

 Watch Out!

Never start a customer profile or questionnaire with touchy demographic questions, such as asking the individual's age or income level. Instead, start with easy-to-answer questions and finish with the more personal queries. That way, if a customer is offended by any questions, at least you have their previous answers.

Picture your perfect customer

Writing a description of your perfect customer can be a very useful exercise. For one, it helps you hone your marketing strategy to better reach that particular group. For another, it can help you see how your current customers differ from the customers you really want to be serving.

After you define your target customer—the type of person likely to be most profitable for your company—you should try to quantify how many such customers there are. Not only will it help you confirm that there is a large enough market to sustain your business, but it will help tremendously in marketing planning, both in establishing a marketing budget and deciding which marketing methods will be most effective.

> ❝ Know your market very, very well. Know what they want. Know where they shop, what they read, radio stations they listen to, TV programs they watch, and where they live. Know everything possible about your market. ❞
>
> —Terri Franklin, owner, Accents of Color

Some of the best reference tools for estimating your target market size are available at your local library, although more are now available online, too. These include the following:

- **The U.S. Census:** www.census.gov
- *Statistical Abstract of the U.S.:* www.census.gov/prod/www/statistical-abstract-04.html
- *County and City Data Book:* www.census.gov/prod/www/ccdb.html
- *State and Metropolitan Area Data Book:* www.census.gov/prod/3/98pubs/smadb-97.pdf
- **Service Annual Survey:** www.census.gov/econ/www/servmenu.html
- *Encyclopedia of Associations:* Available at your local library.

Money Saver

Most local libraries provide access to research databases, such as Dialog and InfoTrac, as long as you have a library card. Before you spend money downloading reports and articles, check with your library to see whether you can get them free.

If you don't find a market size figure that exactly fits what you need, try searching online magazine articles to see whether any publications cite the statistic you're looking for, or if there are reports that reference it. Article databases available at the library generally allow you to search for keywords that match what you're looking for, such as "number of private school students" or "companies with fewer than 200 employees."

If that doesn't work, you'll have to extrapolate from what you have, essentially working backward from what you need based on the data you have in-hand, or combining existing statistics to give you your best guess.

Extrapolating just means you'll need to do some math. For example, you may not be able to find the exact statistic for how many K–12 students there are in the U.S., but you can come up with a strong estimate by adding the number of public school students to the number of parochial and private students. Or, if your product is revolutionary, there is no way you're going to find a published report estimating its market size. However, if you can identify a product with similar functionality or usage benefits, you may be able to use data associated with the other product for your own.

Don't give up if you can't determine the exact size of your target market immediately. It may take a while. But do settle on your best guess based on the information you gather and then refine it over time, as you learn more about your customers and their buying habits.

By constantly tweaking and improving the information you have about your customers, you'll be able to regularly improve the quality of your marketing results. Marketing is an ongoing process, rather than a one-time event, but figuring out who your best customers are or should be is the first step in deciding how best to design your marketing strategy.

Just the facts

- Before you plunk down tons of money to market your product, service, or company, verify that there are enough customers to make your venture profitable.

- Your current customer may not be your best customer. In fact, you may not even want them as customers after you create a profile of your perfect customer and compare the two groups.

- Sometimes, defining a customer by his or her demographic characteristics is inadequate and other factors need to be taken into account, such as psychographics, product or service usage, or geographic location.

- Preparing a customer profile form to evaluate your current customer base can help you more accurately segment your customers and fine-tune your marketing plan.

- There are many tools available, both online and in print, to help you estimate the size of your target market.

- Defining your target market and estimating its total size is a critical first step for developing an effective marketing plan. Without that information, you'll waste money pursuing customers who aren't a good fit for your business.

GET THE SCOOP ON...
Understanding the purchase process ▪ Meeting
customer needs ▪ Highlighting your competitive
advantage ▪ Recognizing pricing pitfalls ▪
Understanding why convenience is key

Why Customers Buy

Chapter 2

The multiple market segments you identify in Chapter 1 are proof that customers buy for different reasons and at different times, places, and price points. Understanding why they buy from you can help you hold on to current customers, do more business with some, and attract new customers—the goal of all your marketing efforts.

Although customers make purchase decisions for different reasons—maybe they saw your product and remembered they needed it, or perhaps they saw work you'd done for another company and wanted to have you do something similar for them—many of the steps in the decision process are the same. Knowing what the steps in the process are and where your potential customer is in that process can be very helpful to landing the sale.

Additionally, understanding how your product or service meets the needs of your target audience, how it compares price-wise to similar products and services, and the major reasons customers buy from you can help you shape your marketing strategy. Your marketing success all starts with zeroing in on why your customers buy—or will buy, in the case of start-up ventures—from you instead of another company.

Decisions, decisions: How customers buy

You know that customers buy for myriad reasons, so here's an overview of how they buy. Understanding that there are five steps to any purchase, and what the steps are, can help you craft marketing messages that speak to people at each stage in the process.

Before a purchase is made, people work through five decision stages: problem recognition, information search, alternative evaluation, purchase decision, and post-purchase behavior. Marketing efforts can impact each stage of the process to increase the chances of a sale, as well as the size of that sale.

Problem recognition

The first stage, problem recognition, is merely the realization that you have a need, whether it's real or perceived. For example, you may see that your car is low on gas, so you head to a service station to buy some. Or maybe a stack of letters to be mailed prompts you to stop by the post office to buy more stamps. These types of needs often become apparent by the absence of something. But needs can also be created through marketing, by suggesting that your life would be made so much better with the purchase of the latest widget. Marketing can make a product or service so appealing that it creates a perceived need—a perceived absence—and in many cases, that's all that is needed to compel someone to buy.

The problem-recognition stage is also relevant in business-to-business settings, where companies may realize they need help meeting a certain timeline or recognize that they don't have the experience on staff to tackle a particular situation.

Information search

After a need has been recognized, consumers typically gather information, reflecting on past purchases or seeking new information from external sources to help in the decision making. Generally, that involves having conversations with family, friends, and colleagues to learn of their experiences with the product or service and to get their recommendations.

Interestingly, a 2001 study conducted by Euro RSCG, cited in *Creating Customer Evangelists,* regarding the purchase of technology products, found that 34 percent of consumers get their information from word-of-mouth (that is, from discussions with others), 20 percent get their information from Web sites, and 13 percent get information from advertisements. That information suggests marketers should be focusing their attention more on generating discussions about their products than on placing ads.

Businesses also gather information and evaluate their options when solving particular problems, which may include creating a Request for Proposal that other companies can respond to, providing their recommended approach to meeting the company's need. Or they may contact companies with which they've done business in the past to get their observations and recommendations. And they turn to the same print and online resources consumers use, to learn all they can about possible solutions.

Alternative evaluation

During the third stage, when customers/prospects evaluate alternatives, they determine what kind of features and benefits are important to them, so that they can compare the various options available. In addition to the product's capabilities or service's promises of performance, other considerations generally include brand name, reputation, prestige, clout, price, and past experience. Weighing all the various considerations, customers eventually make a choice regarding which best meets their current needs.

Purchase decision

The fourth stage is the actual purchase decision. Of course, at this point, customers may decide not to make the purchase at all. Perhaps the item they were considering is more expensive than they wanted to pay, or they decide to put off the decision until a later date. That's one possible course of action.

Businesses are notorious for dragging out purchase decisions for months due to budgetary reasons and other issues, such as the lack of a decision maker. That doesn't mean the purchase won't ever be made, but business-to-business sales cycles are typically much longer than consumer ones.

But when a customer decides to make a purchase, the next decision is deciding where to buy it. Customers browsing in stores are likely to be influenced to make the purchase there, unless given a reason to go elsewhere, such as the price, the attitude of the sales clerk, or the return policy, for example. And if customers are shopping online, they can easily compare several e-tailers.

Selecting the provider for business-to-business products and services often comes down to a group decision based on a set of factors that have been evaluated, or to the decision of the highest ranking person in the room. Assessing the same criteria as consumers consider, businesses then opt to work with a particular supplier.

Post-purchase behavior

After customers make their purchases, they'll either be satisfied with how well it meets their needs, or dissatisfied—the fifth stage in the process. Satisfied customers are likely to become repeat customers and to encourage others to make a similar purchase. They can help generate that valuable word-of-mouth. Conversely, dissatisfied customers are likely to tell others of their dissatisfaction and can potentially derail a company's marketing efforts. For this reason, more companies are following up by phone and e-mail with customers after a sale to reinforce the

Bright Idea

In purchase situations involving high value goods and services, finding ways to reduce the buyer's fear of risk can help seal the deal. Tactics such as offering a performance guarantee, a sample, or extended financing can ease concerns and encourage progress toward the actual purchase.

belief that they made the right choice. And if a problem has come up, the company is alerted sooner rather than later and can potentially fix it and convert the customer to a satisfied buyer.

Although this five-step process is typical, some customers skip over some stages, especially when the decision involves products they frequently purchase, such as groceries or office products, or items that are relatively inexpensive. However, high value products or services, such as multimillion dollar corporate contracts or property purchases, where there is significant concern about making the right choice, may require more evaluation of alternatives and assessment of the options before committing to a purchase.

Your product meets their needs

According to Pamela Danziger, author of *Why People Buy Things They Don't Need*, Americans spend 41 percent of their discretionary income on things they want, but don't necessarily need. That's important information for marketers, who may be overly focused on meeting customer needs.

Obviously, consumers are buying for reasons other than just need. In fact, increasingly, people are buying experiences more than they are buying products or services. They aren't just buying a car to get them from point A to point B, they're buying a feeling of safety or luxury or prestige. Likewise, they don't just buy a stuffed animal, they buy the experience of creating it and helping it come to life, as Build-a-Bear Workshops provide. Today, more than ever, wants and needs are blurred.

When customers buy from you, they are purchasing the perceived benefit of the products or services you offer. For example, they aren't buying a book, they are buying the potential results they will receive from reading it. A diet guide may promise a slimmer physique, and the latest *New York Times* bestseller offers the chance to become engrossed in an entertaining story. By the same token, a corporation doesn't hire a public relations firm to garner more publicity. What they are really after is the impact such publicity will have, including higher sales, enhanced company image, or greater familiarity with their brand.

It all comes down to features and benefits, really. The *feature* is the description of the product or service and how it works. A new car, for example, is made by a particular company, is a sedan or sports car, comes with leather or upholstered seats, and might have XM satellite radio included. These are all features—they describe the components that make up the whole. But the *benefits* are what are really important—they decide which purchase is the best fit for a customer's needs. In the case of a car, the primary benefits have to do with how easily, safely, and quickly it can transport us. Other benefits have to do with how much money we may save versus another car, the prestige factor of investing in a luxury car, or the degree to which the car holds its value over time.

To improve the results of your marketing efforts, think in terms of the benefits your company offers its customers, because customers are benefits focused. They evaluate products and services based on how well the benefits meet their needs.

Your product has a competitive advantage

When customers move into the evaluation phase of the purchase process, they begin comparing their different options. They assess, sometimes feature-by-feature, which offering is the best choice for them. Depending on which factors are most important, they may choose the product or service that offers the most value, the most bang for their buck. Or they may opt for the most expensive choice, putting prestige and brand awareness above all other factors.

The point is, your customers will buy from you for many different reasons. Finding out what their priorities are helps you create marketing messages to encourage them to buy from you and to get the sale. But what makes you really stand out is discovering and developing your own competitive advantage.

A *competitive advantage* is your strength, that one thing that makes you different from your competition and gives customers a reason to choose to do business with you over the others. Some businesses focus on being the low-cost provider in their market and draw price-sensitive shoppers to their door. Other companies emphasize their state-of-the-art equipment and the superior training of their staff, which virtually assures your customers' satisfaction. Service is the theme at some companies, although this can backfire if it suggests that your business's offerings need regular servicing. A large customer base of satisfied clients willing to say good things about your company is another competitive advantage—your company can become the leader based on sheer size and volume.

Your company's strength can become a competitive advantage if customers perceive it to be a big benefit of doing business with you. However, if you elect to promote the fact, for example, that you've been in business for 57 years as your competitive advantage and that's not a decision factor for your customers, then you really don't have an advantage at all.

To find opportunities for creating a competitive advantage, or to discover what customers perceive yours to be, ask them. Take the time to talk with customers regularly and find out what it is about your business that brings them back. Why do they choose to do business with you instead of your competition? Is there a particular feature they love, such as free delivery or online access to their information? Find out what it is, and then incorporate it into your marketing message.

Watch Out!

A competitive advantage can lead to increased sales, but only if customers perceive it to be a competitive advantage and are aware of it. Be sure all potential customers are aware of the advantages of your products and services.

Your product is priced right

Some customers are extremely price-focused, which means their purchase decisions are guided almost entirely by the comparative price of items they need or want. It is apt to be a pivotal factor in the decision to purchase, although that doesn't mean it's the only factor, or even the deciding factor.

To make sure your company's offerings are seriously considered, evaluate your pricing strategy to make sure it matches your target market. Selling commodities for prices well above the market rate will be just as ineffective as quoting your hourly fee well below the going rate for your services. Remind yourself of your target customer's profile as you assess how you've set the pricing of your products and services.

There are three general pricing strategies that companies use to price their products; review these to make sure your prices are in line with your customers' expectations. The pricing strategy you use will impact your marketing and can help or hurt your efforts to attract and keep customers.

Cost + markup

The first strategy is based on the actual cost of the product or service, plus a standard percentage markup. This is standard procedure in some industries, with the downside being that profits are limited.

Market-based

Another strategy is a *market-based* one, in which the price is set according to what other players in the market are charging. Companies research and monitor what competitors are charging for similar products and services and price theirs accordingly. However, all businesses should know their cost basis, even if they don't price that way, to be sure that the market price is enough to cover their expenses. Your *cost basis* is how much it costs your company to produce one unit of your product or service. In order to be profitable, to make money, you need to know what it costs to stay in business. For example, if it costs your firm $72 an hour for an architect to work on a project, based on salary, benefits, and overhead, and the going rate in your area is a rate of $70 an hour, you would lose $2 an hour on every customer project if you charged the market rate. If you're pricing based on what others in your market are charging, make sure that amount is, at the very least, above your cost.

Perceived pricing strategy

Thirdly, you can use a *perceived value pricing strategy,* in which you charge an amount based on the value the customer places on your offerings. Many consultants advocate using this strategy, which can potentially generate more revenue, but be aware that it can also price you out of the market. Perceived value pricing works in situations in which a product or service experiences a huge spike in demand, to the point that demand exceeds supply. A recent example of perceived value pricing is occurring with hybrid vehicles, which are being sold above the sticker price to consumers who want them badly! Those scrambling to buy the product offer larger and larger sums of money to be able to obtain it.

 Bright Idea

Paco Underhill, author of *Why People Buy,* reports that in retail environments, the more shopper-employee interaction, the larger the ultimate sale. Apply that theory to your own business and increase the amount of contact you and your employees have with your customers.

Your product is convenient

Many time-starved consumers are heavily influenced by convenience when making a purchase decision. Considerations like how long it will take to get to your location, how late you are open (or what time you open your doors), how easy it is to get in and out of your location, whether parking is free and close by, whether the purchase will free up time to do something else, and whether it will eliminate some other required—perhaps disliked—activity are all factors. Just look at the skyrocketing sales of prepared meals at the grocery store and increasingly popular curbside take-out service at even modestly-priced restaurants; consumers want products and services that allow them to get more done in the day, perhaps by skipping cooking dinner.

Recognizing that convenience is key for many consumers, and for businesses, too, think of ways to highlight how convenient it is to do business with you. Do you pick up and drop off documents from your corporate clients, provide 24-hour accessibility and service, give routine end-of-day status reports, or offer free answers to (brief) questions by phone? All of these features provide the one major benefit today's customer wants: convenience. The more you can make it easier for someone—an individual or business client—to do business with you, the more business you will earn.

Make a list of all the ways your products or services offer greater convenience than competitors', or brainstorm new levels of convenience you can offer. These might include

- **Extended work hours:** Open earlier, close later
- **Unlimited phone access:** No additional charge for phone calls from your location
- **Direct phone line to a live voice:** Avoid the automated runaround
- **Faster turnaround/completion:** Speedier delivery of projects
- **Delivery and/or pick up:** For free or a fee
- **Access to information online:** Password-protected Web site

- **Personalized advice:** Knowledgeable consultants who can help customers avoid a poor purchase choice

- **Previews of upcoming sales or promotions:** Advanced warning or special deals only for the best customers

- **Financing options:** Only a percentage down; extended payment terms

- **Payment flexibility:** A house tab or check acceptance

As consumers increasingly rate time as more valuable than money, convenience has become a major factor in the purchase decision. The more convenience you can build into your business, the more attractive you become to your customers.

Just the facts

- There are as many reasons why customers buy as there are market segments. For that reason, you'll want to give your target market plenty of reasons to buy from you.

- Customers move through a five-step process when considering a purchase, from problem recognition to information search to alternative evaluation to purchase decision and to post-purchase behavior. Some of these steps are skipped with low-risk, high-frequency purchases, while other steps can be extended when high-value, high-risk purchases are being considered.

- How well your offering meets the needs of your customers is a key factor in the decision process, although today there is more of an emphasis on benefits than on features—customers are interested in the whole experience associated with the product or service.

- You can create a competitive advantage that attracts customers by identifying your perceived strengths and leveraging that throughout your marketing efforts. Find out why customers buy from you in order to capitalize on that advantage.

- Ensuring that your products and services are priced properly is another way to increase sales. Look carefully at your cost structure and your competitor's pricing strategy to determine which pricing approach will best appeal to customers.

- Convenience has become a major factor in the purchase decision, with companies seeing their sales soar when they build convenience into their products and services. Evaluate how you can make it less time-consuming and more convenient for customers to do business with you.

Know Your Enemies

Chapter 3

Focusing too much time and energy on what the competition is doing takes your attention away from your own business, which can be deadly. Too many major corporations have fallen on hard times as a result of trying to one-up their closest competitors, when they might have actually succeeded if they had instead paid more attention to showcasing the ways in which their own company was special.

Although paying too much attention to your competitors can be dangerous, pretending they don't exist is equally foolish. You don't want to mimic the marketing efforts of your competitors exactly, but you also don't want to ignore their presence and let them steal your customers.

Fortunately, there is a happy medium, where small businesses routinely monitor their competition, study their marketing methods, assess their sales success, and implement improvements—without becoming obsessed with beating them.

Studying how other businesses in your industry are marketing themselves is smart. Similar to a *best practices* effort, in which you identify the best policies,

Bright Idea

Call (or have a colleague call) each of your competitors and request an information packet. Look at the type of information they send prospective customers to assess how big a threat they are to your business. Are the materials impressive? Are they amateurish? How do yours compare?

procedures, and marketing methods other companies are using, gathering competitor intelligence helps you become familiar with your competitors' strengths and weaknesses. That information is key to developing a marketing program that helps you attract all the high-profit business you can handle.

Who are they?

The first step in studying your competition is to create a list of all the companies you know or suspect may compete with you for your target customers. In fact, if you're starting a new business, it may help to start with a list of types of businesses you think compete with yours, and then seek out company names within those categories—the phone book (in print or online) is always a good place to start if you are locally focused.

Your competitors may be in the same industry or they may be in a totally different type of business but also offer your particular service or products. An example of this situation is the pet-grooming market, where a number of different types of businesses—veterinary offices, pet supply chains, mobile pet-grooming vans, and retail pet grooming locations—all offer pet grooming. All of these types of businesses compete for the same customers, so they are all competitors.

If your business is local, you'll want to prepare a complete list of businesses in your area that attract your customers; unless your customers would buy from a business out-of-state, you don't need to concern yourself with them. For example, if you run a mortgage brokerage firm, your territory is probably limited by your geography. But if your clientele includes international corporations that frequently hire consultants from far-flung cities, your geography is not a factor in the buying process and you shouldn't use it to limit your definition of your competition. Your competitors could be across town or on another continent.

For help in finding out who you may be competing with, here are some free or low-cost tools to scope out the competition:

- **www.yellowpages.com:** Start with the simplest source of all, the Yellow Pages online, and search for companies within your industry or category.

- **www.google.com:** Type in key words you would expect customers to use to find your business and see which company names pop up. '

- **www.tgrnet.com:** Search the *Thomas Register* online to find information about more than 700,000 industrial product and service companies.

- **www.bizweb.com:** Search the more than 46,000 company listings in 200+ categories at this Web site, which tends to have more small business listings than large.

- **www.hoovers.com:** Utilize this subscription service to research public companies for an annual fee—the higher the fee you pay, the more ways you can use the information on the site, such as creating mailing lists.

- **Professional associations:** Membership in your industry association(s) frequently includes a member directory, which can help you pinpoint all your competitors.

Bright Idea

If your company often bids on customer jobs, take the opportunity to ask your contact, or the purchasing agent, which other companies placed a bid. You may discover some new names you weren't aware of. Start monitoring these companies.

Sometimes, your biggest competitor may not even have shown up on your initial list. You may not have heard about a new business that just opened up a few miles away, an existing company that has recently added to its product selection, or an unrelated business that is testing the waters in your industry. But competitor research will help you ferret out the latest information to help you make better decisions about how to spend your marketing dollars.

What do they offer?

As you study your competitors, add to your marketing assessment a checklist or tally that keeps track of what they do and don't sell, how they sell it (through what channels of distribution), and how their pricing stacks up to yours. In all, this checklist covers the four Ps of marketing: product, place, price, and promotion, which are the fundamentals.

An outline of your checklist might include some or all of the following information for each competitor:

Competitor Profile

Company name

Headquarters address

Local address

Phone number

Web site URL

Key contacts internally

Annual sales

Profit margin (as a dollar value or percentage)

Number of employees

Number of divisions or business units

Names of divisions

Number of branch offices or locations

Market share percentage

Number of dealers

Number of distributors

Number of technical support/service employees

Target markets

New product introductions

Size of subscriber base

Key accounts/clients

Target market

Technology platform

Pricing strategy (per hour rate/project basis)

Unique selling proposition

Size of marketing budget

Largest marketing expenditure

 Money Saver

To track what your competitors are up to, register online for a free news service at www.individual.com. After typing in information about the topics and companies you want to monitor, you'll begin receiving news bulletins via e-mail regarding your industry and competitors.

How do they measure up?

When you know who your competition is and have a sense of how they are marketing their companies, you can get serious about assessing them. In other words, you want to be brutally honest in comparing your company's offerings to those of your competitors in order to understand how to market your business and come out the winner.

Some of the aspects to look at include the following:

- Financial resources
- Management talent
- Manufacturing capacity
- Distribution network/channels
- Supplier relationships
- Marketing prowess
- Trends and forecasts (is the business improving or declining?)

One way to compare and contrast your company with others is to set up a spreadsheet or a grid, with the companies listed across the top and the characteristics you're evaluating listed down the side. Then you can use a rudimentary system such as +, −, and N (for neutral) as a general indicator of how you stack up.

	Company A	Company B	Company C
Financial resources			
Management talent			
Manufacturing capacity			
Distribution network/ channels			
Supplier relationships			
Marketing prowess			
Trends and forecasts			

Understanding your company's strengths and weaknesses will help you make the best decisions to give your company a competitive edge.

Bright Idea

If you're having trouble tracking down information about a certain company, including their sales figures, you might want to consider paying Dun & Bradstreet for a credit report. For around $140 at www.dnb.com/us, an official credit report can tell you about a company's financial strength, payment history, major customers, and primary lines of business.

What's their marketing strategy?

To understand how your competitors are carving out their own niche and positioning themselves for the business they are getting, study their marketing approach. Gather examples of their marketing. Spend a little time tracking down evidence of their marketing efforts, such as the following:

- Advertisements (print, broadcast, and Web)
- Articles (in newspapers, magazines, and newsletters, and on the Internet)
- Billboards
- Brochures and other literature
- Bus signage/ads (interior and exterior)
- Business cards
- E-mail offers or contacts
- Listserv discussions (customer comments, rumors)
- News announcements (press releases, bulletins, media advisories)
- Newsletters (electronic and print)
- Product catalog (electronic and print)
- Professional or trade association involvement
- Promotional giveaways
- Sales incentives (coupons, flyers, and other offers)
- Signs
- Speaking engagements

Money Saver

College- or MBA-level marketing classes can be a great, low-cost way of tackling large marketing projects. Instead of trying to accomplish such a project yourself, call the marketing department chair at a local college to ask whether the department has an upcoming class that might be able to take it on as part of a class project for credit.

- Sponsorships of events
- Stationery
- Web site (home page layout, navigation, links to other sites, and so on)

As you look through all of your competitors' materials, what kind of image do you have of the company? Make note of the initial impression you get, which is what customers may also be thinking. Try to develop a description of the company's personality or image by answering the following questions:

- Is it upscale or inexpensive?
- What type of customer is it targeting?
- Does the company seem trustworthy, or does it sound a little too good to be true?
- Are the materials professional or hokey?
- Do the marketing materials look like they all came from the same company, or from several different ones?
- Does it use several marketing methods, or rely on just one or two?
- Do its ads and brochures look homemade or professionally prepared?
- What types of photos does it use—professional or amateur?
- Is the company Internet-savvy or not?
- Does the company look like it's doing well, or does it appear to be struggling?

Watch Out!

Be aware that the tactics you're using to learn about your competitors' plans can also be used against you, to monitor your plans. Make every effort to keep your marketing activities private, or you may lose your advantage.

- What are its primary products and services?
- Would you guess that the company charges a premium, or is it the low-cost provider?
- How many locations does it have?
- What is its geographic service area, or focus?
- Is it a large operation or small?
- Does it appear to be very experienced and knowledgeable, or new to the business?
- What one word would you use to describe the company?
- Would you do business with the company?

Because marketing tools are often a customer's first experience with a company, they shape the first impression. And that first impression can determine whether the company ultimately gets the customer's business. What kind of first impression do each of your competitors give? How does that compare to your company's first impression? Are changes needed?

Take an inside look at their operations

There are a number of strategies for gathering information on companies, and they fall into two general categories: primary research and secondary research.

Primary research

Primary research is first-hand information gathering, either by personal observation or interaction. Because you're doing all the work, primary research is generally more time consuming and expensive than secondary research (see the following section), but sometimes you'll uncover information no one else has noticed.

Sometimes the most important information is the easiest to get, simply by paying attention. For example, using the technique of observation, you can learn a lot about an organization. By traveling to your competitor's place of business, you may be able to determine the following:

- Number of employees, based on the number of parking spaces in the parking lot

- Amount of merchandise or raw materials purchased per week, by counting the number of delivery trucks making deliveries in that time period

- Who its major suppliers are, by noting the names on the trucks and vans that visit the building

- Number of customers per hour, or per day, by counting how many customers go in and out in that time frame

- Approximate sales, by counting how many customers come out carrying purchases

- Demographic profile of its customer base, by tracking who is coming and going

The preceding list is a simple starting point to get you thinking about what you could learn if you studied your competitor first-hand—there are certainly many additional pieces of information to be gathered.

On top of observation, you can also do some digging in court documents and filings, primarily to learn more about the company's properties and plans for expansion or consolidation, based on any filings made with the local town or county. Local courts should be able to provide basic information about any lawsuits filed locally as well.

Taking photographs is always smart, too, if you're permitted. Many retailers, for example, no longer allow individuals to take photographs inside, but that doesn't mean you can't take exterior photos.

Finally, don't ignore the power of conversation. Pleasantries exchanged with suppliers, mutual acquaintances, customers, and your own employees can yield a wealth of information about your competitor's plans. The grapevine is alive and well and can be a superb source of useful information.

Secondary research

Secondary research relies on existing, published information on which to base your assessment. Common tools for this kind of research include newspaper articles, magazine articles, reports, studies, newsletters, white papers, and other published documents. Secondary research is typically faster and easier to conduct than primary research because it's really more of an information-gathering task.

You can easily start your information gathering using secondary research. Some online tools you may want to check into include

- **ABI/Inform:** A database accessible primarily through schools and libraries, which provides business and management information.

- **www.fuld.com/TIndex/IntelOrg.html:** The Intelligence Organizer at this site helps you identify the specific information you need in order to understand your competitors' advantages.

- **www.hoovers.com:** Sign up for Hoovers Lite and receive access to the database of 40,000 public companies in the United States.

- **www.proquest.com:** Used by students, faculty, and staff to prepare research papers, this database can be a valuable tool for studies and reports.

- **www.sec.gov:** Scan filings from public companies using the Securities and Exchange Commission's EDGAR database.

- **http://globaledge.msu.edu:** Businesses interested in exploring opportunities, as well as competitors, outside the United States should check out this Web site for global guidance from Michigan State University's Center for International Business Education and Research.

Leonard Fuld, author of the book *Competitor Intelligence,* considered the bible of the field, suggests the following additional sources:

- Industry directories
- State corporate filings
- Management biographies
- Trade shows
- Environmental-impact statements
- Classified/help-wanted ads
- Research and development sources
- Buyers' guides
- City directories

Keep in mind that it's unlikely you'll find exactly what you're looking for all in one place—rarely is it that easy. For example, if you're trying to find out which direction a competitor is headed product-development-wise, the company may not reveal it directly, but you may be able to piece it together from newspaper help-wanted ads looking for a particular expertise, local property transfer records, and conversations with some of your suppliers, who confirm the company has been buying a lot more of a particular raw material. Or if you've heard a company is up for sale, your competitor may not confirm it, but a call to a local business broker, or a visit to a national business brokerage Web site, may give you the answer.

The best information usually results from a combination of primary and secondary research, rather than one or the other.

Bright Idea

If your biggest competitor is out of your area, subscribe to the local newspaper in that company's city or regularly check the online edition to keep tabs on the company. Sometimes, companies reveal information about their plans to the local media, which you would normally miss out on if you were monitoring only the national media.

Information is power

In any business situation, more information is always better than less. The more you know about your competition, the greater the advantage you'll have in developing your own marketing plan, carving out your own niche, and strengthening your company's capabilities. You'll be in a better negotiating position with your vendors, employment candidates, landlord, and even your customers when you know more about what your competitor is paying and charging.

Recognizing your own strengths and weaknesses can help you make smarter, more informed business decisions, ramping up in certain areas or scaling back in others based on what you know about the market. Rarely will you be caught off-guard if you develop a competitor intelligence system and invest time regularly to check on your major competitors. Shop their stores, interview their managers, chat with their customers, and speak with their suppliers to learn all you can about what they're up to. Your business will be better off for it.

Just the facts

- Whether you want to admit it or not, you have competitors, and those competitors impact who buys from you and when. However, that doesn't mean you should develop your marketing approach as a reaction to your competition. You shouldn't. But you should be aware of what they're up to.

- Find out who your competitors really are and aren't—the results may be surprising. Through your research (such as by asking your customers directly), you may discover that the companies you thought you competed with really aren't a threat, and that other players are the ones frequently considered alongside you. That's important information that may change your marketing approach.

- Spend some time studying how your competitors market themselves. Gather as many examples of their marketing efforts and assess the kind of image they present. How is yours different? How can you improve it?

- Evaluate your competition's marketing efforts to determine where it is strong and where it is weak. Finding out its strengths helps you craft a marketing message that makes you stand out. You'll want to hit hard where your competitor is weak, but you first need to figure out what each competitor's weakness is.

- There are low-cost tools available to monitor what your competitors are up to on an ongoing basis—recent hires, new product developments, or financial maneuvers—that can help you stay one step ahead of them.

- Information gathered based on both primary (first-hand) research and secondary (existing, publicly available) data is typically the most complete and accurate.

Planning Your Success

GET THE SCOOP ON...
Creating the best image for your company ▪
Carving out your market position ▪ Developing
popular positioning strategies ▪ Defining your
competitive advantage

Positioning

Chapter 4

Market positioning is what makes one brand different from another in the minds of buyers. One may be the higher-quality option, while another may be known for its service, innovation, or a quirky added benefit. Positioning shapes the perception consumers have of the brand and the product, with a goal of appealing to more buyers and increasing sales. Two products or services may be essentially the same but can be positioned as completely different.

Take Volvo, for example. Marketers there have positioned its cars as extremely safe and durable, while Mercedes-Benz, a similar upscale automobile, has emphasized more of the luxury aspect of its line of cars. BMW, on the other hand, is positioned as a high-performance auto—"the ultimate driving machine." All three brands are well known, well respected, and very reliable, but the different information provided about each has influenced how consumers think about them. That differentiation has occurred thanks to market positioning.

Perception is reality

It really doesn't matter which product or service is truly superior to another because positioning

Bright Idea

If, through your marketing message, you can convince buyers that your company has the hottest offerings, or the most exclusive, reliable, best value—whatever benefits you want to use—people will begin to believe the information and see your product in a certain light. As a result, competing products will also be viewed in a new light relative to yours.

changes everything. A strong marketing campaign to position your product or service as having certain attributes or benefits can upset a level playing field.

Take soap, for example. Several years ago, in response to heightened concerns about germs and bacteria, a few brands of soap began marketing themselves as "antibacterial," or having the ability to kill more than 99 percent of all bacteria on your hands. The message was a hit with nervous consumers eager to rid their households of enemy germs; sales of those products rose relative to the competition.

The funny thing is that soaps are, by definition, antibacterial. That's what they are meant to do—get rid of dirt and germs. So calling a soap brand "antibacterial" is redundant, but it resonated with buyers, who wanted reassurance that using soap would help eradicate a health threat. That process is what positioning is all about—persuading buyers to buy from you by emphasizing or creating a competitive advantage that places your company in a positive light.

Who's on first?

So that your products or services are perceived as having attributes or benefits that are superior to your competitors', choose a market position that addresses buyer concerns. As you brainstorm potential positions your product or services could take, consider some of the following:

▪ What prompts buyers to purchase your product or service? Is there a certain event that generates a need?

Watch Out!

Companies that are the clear market leader, even on a local level, should be careful when bragging about being number one. Some customers are turned off by companies that pat themselves on the back. It's okay to state your leadership position, especially if you can tie it to a specific customer benefit, but don't use your heightened status to put down the competition.

- What are the top purchase criteria buyers use in choosing which brand to buy? For example, are they most concerned with reliability? price? after-sales service? your return policy? What is it that can make or break a sale?

- Do you serve a limited geographic area, or are you national or international in your scope?

- What are your company's, or brand's, strengths?

- What are your company's weaknesses, as perceived by your customers?

- How would you like customers to think of your company or its offerings?

- How would you like customers to think of your prices— bargain basement, expensive but worth it, or very competitive?

- If you could change one misperception of your company, what would it be?

What makes you different?

The major characteristics on which companies differentiate and position themselves include the following:

- **Price:** How your product or service is priced relative to similar products and services says a lot about your market position. Is your company aiming to be the low-cost provider? Or are you trying to stay right in the middle, meeting the needs of customers who want a good value, but don't necessarily need to pay the lowest possible price.

Or are you targeting the upper end of the market, where paying a higher price is not a deterrent to a purchase and, in some cases, may actually boost sales?

■ **Quality:** How does the quality of your work or your product compare? Are you known for the best workmanship? Is one of your company's priorities product or service quality? Or is some failure acceptable because the price is so low? Where your company falls on the quality continuum can determine your position.

■ **Service:** Is after-sales service part of your positioning? Do you provide service bundled as part of customer purchases, to make sure they make full use of your offerings? Do you offer free phone support? Do you accept returns without question? Your attitude toward service and how much you're willing to provide is another potential source of differentiation and positioning.

■ **Channels of distribution:** How you distribute your product or service is another way to position your offerings because channels shape consumer perception. Being able to buy your product via the Internet says one thing about your company, while seeing it on a TV infomercial may say another. Where your product or service can be purchased influences your market position.

■ **Packaging:** How your product or service is *packaged*—how it is delivered to your customer—can also impact the perception of your offerings. Expensive, upscale paper and rich colors suggest one thing about your consulting services, for example, while a brown paper bag with a hand-stamped logo says something else, and both help establish customer perceptions regarding your company.

The key to success is to identify what your strength is and use it as the basis for your market position. Don't try to be all things to all customers, or to differentiate yourself on every possible factor, such as pricing, quality, service, distribution, *and* packaging.

Instead, focus on one element and be known for that—your unique selling proposition.

Positioning strategies

After you've decided what makes your product or service unique, or at least different from competitors, it's time to select a positioning strategy—essentially, why customers should buy from you instead of from someone else. There are six basic strategies to choose from in answering that question:

- **Product features:** Is there a feature only your product has that customers have decided is valuable? This could be anything from a capability no other product on the market has, such as being made from a certain material, like aluminum, or perhaps being free of others, such as fat. An attribute could be a certain level of performance, such as output capacity or computing speed. Or it could be speed of delivery, which is especially important with services.

- **Product benefits:** Similarly, does your product or service provide benefits that no other does? For example, do you offer free lifetime service on your product? Can you guarantee a certain level of reliability or performance? The results or benefits from using your product or service are an excellent choice for a positioning strategy because most customers buy in order to reap a product's or service's benefits.

- **Usage occasions:** Another strategy is to position your product or service as perfect for a particular event or occasion. That could be anything from a special occasion, such as a wedding or first baby, to a more common occurrence, such as whenever you vacuum your carpeting or when "It's Miller Time." Suggesting that customers buy from you when they have a particular need, such as "When it's midnight and your computer crashes," can be an effective strategy because it helps customers know when to call. When there are specific instances that your product or service is a perfect fit, remind customers of those instances.

- **User groups:** Another way to position your company's offerings is by specifying which type of customer you serve, or which types of users will benefit most from working with you. User groups could be demographic, such as based on gender, age, or income level, or they could be based on a connection to a particular company or activity, such as a hobby. For example, AARP is for consumers age 50 and over, while McDonald's Happy Meals are for young children.

- **Against a competitor:** Comparing your offerings directly to a competitor can sometimes work. The classic example of this strategy is Avis car rentals, which states that because it is number two in the market, it tries harder to satisfy its customers. Avis suggests you'll get better service than from its major competitor because it's not a megacorporation. Although Avis doesn't state the name of its competitor, the company makes clear what its position is: number two and proud of it!

- **Away from a competitor:** Of course, when a competitor is in turmoil or has a tarnished reputation, you want to make sure your company is not lumped together with your brethren. By distancing yourself from the competition, you can hope to avoid any collateral damage. When you hear, "Unlike other XX stores, we don't . . . ," you know this is the positioning strategy the company has adopted.

Holding on to the lead

According to Al Ries and Jack Trout, authors of *Positioning: The Battle for Your Mind,* the market leader in a product category typically has twice the market share of the second largest competitor, which has twice the market share of the third largest competitor. Being first in a product category provides a significant advantage—a lead that others companies will have difficulty overcoming.

Bright Idea

Choosing a brand name is one of the most important decisions your company will likely make, impacting buyer perceptions of the product it is associated with. Because consumers are barraged with product and brand names, choose one that describes what it is associated with, such as Gleem toothpaste or Chunky Soup, rather than a generic word that has no link to the product or service.

However, leaders are not impenetrable. If you currently hold the number one position in your market, be aware of the large lead you have over your competition, but don't take it for granted.

To expand your business, develop new brands to compete in other markets, but don't try to slap your leading brand on a multitude of products and expect that they'll also be successful. Take Gerber Singles, for example, a single-serving adult product the baby food company thought would do well with senior citizens. Instead, consumers thought they were trying to sell baby food to adults. It didn't work. A better strategy for Gerber would have been to create an entirely new brand. Rather than spreading your bread-and-butter brand too thin, or applying it to an unrelated product or service, create a new brand.

Product line extensions (that is, when you apply a known brand name to a new product) generally work only when the new product is very closely related to the existing brand—such as the new custom-colored M&Ms or the multitude of Swiffer products, all of which remove household dust. Extensions that expect buyers to make a leap to a new use, a new flavor, or an entirely new service are much more risky.

The follower advantage

Being second in a market isn't all bad, but it's better to be first to market if you can. Once stuck in second, the key to success is finding a position that isn't already claimed by the leader. For

Watch Out!

Just don't try to go head to head with a runaway leader in your field. You'll likely lose because of your competitor's substantial lead. Simply differentiate yourself so that customers understand the advantage of buying from your company.

example, if your competitor has designated itself as the family-friendly amusement park, perhaps your park could be teen-oriented, or for adults. Or if the leading copy shop has decided it wants to be a second home for small businesses, perhaps your shop can go after corporate work or educational institutions. If the work is there, you can be just as profitable, and maybe more so, than the leader.

Just the facts

- Positioning your product or service in a particular way involves shaping consumer perception.

- Customer perceptions may not be accurate, and that's what buyers rely on to make choices. If perceptions of your brand are negatively skewed, you need to reposition your products or services to persuade customers to buy.

- Companies can use price, quality, service, channels of distribution, or packaging as the basis of differentiation in positioning.

- There are six positioning strategies companies can use to differentiate a product or service from existing offerings. Using product features, benefits, usage occasions, or user groups; comparing against a competitor; or distancing the offering from the competition can all yield success.

GET THE SCOOP ON...
Recognizing the importance of an action plan ■
Exploring the financial benefits of goal setting ■
Setting attainable goals ■ Prioritizing ■ Tracking
your progress and success

Goal Setting

Chapter 5

If you've ever set a personal, business, or financial goal, you're probably already familiar with the benefits of goal setting. But you may not realize that the same process works just as well in marketing your small business.

By stating your goal—your target—and then breaking down that larger objective into smaller tasks, you can make steady progress to achieve it. This works for just about any aspect of business management, and is especially useful in marketing.

The bottom line

The whole point of setting goals for your marketing efforts is to help you decide where to invest the bulk of your time, effort, and marketing money. Your goal(s) become your mission, your lightning rod, and help ensure that everything you do on a daily basis is bringing you closer to achieving your stated goals.

In general, goal setting works by having you define a large, perhaps long-term goal, and then slowly break it down into mid-sized activities, then

Watch Out!

Although your focus in goal setting is presumably on the results you hope to achieve, be careful how you state your goals. Make sure they are within your control. You can do this by expressing them in terms of outputs, not outcomes. That is, write them in terms of what you can do to improve the odds of reaching your goals, rather than what you'd like to have happen—you have little control over that and may get frustrated if you don't reach your goals.

those into smaller activities, and then each of those into daily tasks. But you start with the end in mind—your goals.

Picturing the future

To begin, envision what you want your company to look like in the next three or five years—what I call the *long-term*. Picture some of the following, five years hence:

- Where is the company located? in a home office? in cushy commercial space? in a foreign country?

- How many employees do you have? one? five? one-hundred?

- What kinds of clients or customers are you serving, primarily? major corporations? neighborhood families? relocating military service members?

- How much money is the company making? $100,000 a year? $500,000 a year? $3 million? more?

- What one word describes your reputation or image? experts? bargain? convenient? delicious? It all depends on your type of business, of course, but what is your market position?

When you have a picture (albeit fuzzy) of what you want your company to look like in the future, jot down four or five goals. One should be a financial one, because success is often defined by the amount of business the company is doing, and the other goals should reflect your business priorities. If you're

Bright Idea

Use the technique of visualization to help you create an image of what you want your company to be like in the future. Picturing in your own mind what a successful company—your successful company—looks like can make it easier to set goals that will have a major impact on your company's ultimate success. After you can picture it, you can determine what you need to do to make the fantasy a reality.

just getting started, you may want to have an established base of 200 regular customers, for example. Or, if you're in growth mode, maybe a better gauge would be a percentage increase in the number of individual client engagements you have, or sales transactions per month. Securing outside investors or being elected president of the local professional association for your industry may be a long-term goal. It's up to you to decide what you want your business to look like in the coming years.

Preparing effective goals

Here are some general guidelines to help you create effective marketing-related goals:

- **Express your goals positively, not negatively.** Rather than attempting to stop certain behaviors, for example, such as taking on any client, without regard to budget, focus instead on what you will do, such as pursue more high-income customers.

- **State your goal precisely.** If your aim is to increase your number of customers, write your goal in terms of a specific number of new customers in a particular time frame, such as "land two new customers per month." Or set a clear deadline for yourself. "March 31st," for example, is precise, while "by the second quarter" leaves a wide margin for error and gives you an excuse to procrastinate. Use numbers whenever possible.

- **Focus on your level of performance.** Your performance is typically within your control, but what occurs as a result is not. For example, if your goal is to generate new business from area business leaders, you may choose to speak once a month at area business organizations. That's a performance goal. Granted, it's very likely that new business will result, but you can't set new business goals based on your public speaking efforts, because there is no way to tell how much new business may come in.

- **Keep the goals realistic.** It's great to have lofty dreams, but shooting too high can negatively impact your performance. A goal that is so far out of reach in the short term, or even the long term, can become frustrating and demoralizing. But a goal that can be achieved within your set time frame, whether it is one year or five years, keeps you motivated because you know it is within your grasp.

- **Prioritize.** After you've established your goals, rank them in order of priority—from most important to least important. Making decisions about marketing strategies and tactics will be much easier if your goals are not given equal merit. For example, increasing your sales by 20 percent this year will likely be much more important than starting a blog, which generally wouldn't have as significant an impact on sales as other methods. Therefore, the sales increase goal should be of higher priority.

- **Put it in writing.** Studies have shown that the act of writing goals helps strengthen your commitment to achieving them and may even trigger your subconscious mind to begin formulating how best to get results. Plus, unless your goals are in writing, you'll have a tough time revisiting your plans and thoughts.

- **Set a completion date.** Someone once said, "goals are dreams with a deadline." Until you commit to reaching your goal within a certain time frame, it's difficult to break

Watch Out!

An oft-cited Harvard Business School study, comparing 1979 graduates ten years after graduation, reported that only 3 percent of the grads wrote down their goals. Another 14 percent had goals, but didn't write them down. And 83 percent did not even have well-defined goals. But what's really interesting is that the 3 percent with written goals earned ten times that of the 83 percent who didn't set goals.

down what you need to do on a monthly, weekly, or daily basis, because you haven't determined how much time you're working with.

▪ **Make sure your goals are challenging.** Setting goals that you are sure you can achieve in short order is a waste of time. The whole purpose of goal setting is to get you to stretch as a leader and as a company. Part of the process of goal setting involves imagining what is possible for your company, and then determining how to make it happen. If you are already in the process of making it happen, you don't need to state it as a goal. Choose a more difficult one instead.

The next step: Making action plans

After defining your marketing goals, your next task is to break them down into individual steps you can tackle in little chunks, such as in 15 minutes or an hour.

Start by identifying the key steps you need to take to reach each goal. For example, if increasing sales by 50 percent this year is a goal, your key steps may be as follows:

▪ Evaluate marketing program for previous year.

▪ Identify methods that generated the largest amount of new or incremental business.

▪ Finalize marketing budget for current year.

There might also be other steps, depending on how much information you have about your marketing results in the past.

Money Saver

For help in creating an action plan, download a free template, created by Deborah Crawford of BellaOnline, at www.smart-marketing-works.com/action-plans.html. It will help you identify your goal, actions steps, measurable results, target completion date, and a results column.

After you have a first level of action steps, you'll want to break each of those three key steps down further.

If need be, break that second level of actions down further, and continue until you have brief steps that could be completed in one day or less. Now schedule all of those activities in the coming weeks, keeping in mind the target completion date for your goal.

In the case of this example, your completion date would presumably be the end of your company's fiscal year, which may also be the calendar year. So your due date is December 31. But the sooner you complete your tasks, the sooner those marketing programs will start to have an impact on sales.

Staying on track

Although setting goals is the tough part, the real value of goal setting comes after the fact—once you start to use your goals to track your progress.

Unless you take the time to state where your company is headed, it's nearly impossible to judge how well it is doing. If revenues are growing at 10 percent a year, to some business owners that would be terrific news, because their businesses only grew 4 percent. But unless you had stated a revenue goal for the year, it's hard to judge whether you had a successful year. However, if you'd set a goal at the beginning of the year to achieve 9 percent growth and you were able to reach 10 percent, you'd have cause for celebration. You did it!

Goals also allow you to assess how well things are going. And sometimes they require modification mid-stream. Perhaps one of your goals is to win some business from a major national corporation, such as Microsoft or American Express. So you developed an action plan with regular activities that will ultimately get your foot in the door and, eventually, some business. But if one of the companies suddenly announces a major new initiative in your area of expertise, you may want to ramp up your contact with them to jump on the opportunity. And your goal may change.

The best way to stay on track with your goals is to post them where you'll see them regularly. You may also want to attach your action plan to your marketing plan, so that you can be sure your marketing efforts are supporting your marketing and business priorities. And if you have employees, you'll want to share your goals with them and get their input and buy-in, to significantly increase the odds of your business's reaching them.

Refer to your goals daily, if possible, or at least weekly, to see what action items you have to tackle next week, and to review the progress you made the previous week. As you complete your action steps, you'll be on your way to reaching your goals.

Financial goals

Setting goals that are quantifiable—expressed as numbers—makes it easier to track your progress. And because financial figures are, by definition, numbers, let's start some goal setting using financial *metrics,* or measures.

Using the preceding guidelines for crafting useful goals, let's apply them to marketing activities that impact the bottom line. These could include goals having to do with the following:

- Increase in total dollar sales
- Percentage growth in sales
- Increase in average transaction value
- Increase in frequency of purchase
- Decrease in marketing expenses
- Positive *return on investment* (ROI)—a percentage representing the amount of money made for each $1 spent on marketing. A positive ROI means that your $1 investment in marketing generated *more* than $1 in sales.

- Increase in *profit margin* (the amount you've earned over and above your expenses)
- Merchandise turnover rate
- Number of billed hours

Depending on your type of business and industry, there may be other financial goals that are particularly relevant—but don't let financial goals be the only ones you consider.

Customer goals

Financial performance is often used as the first measure of a company's marketing success, but customers always make or break a business—customers choose to spend their money with your company or with a competitor.

But because the link between marketing and sales is not direct, meaning that it's often difficult to attribute a particular financial result to an individual marketing campaign, you may want to set customer-related goals, which have more of a causal link with marketing. Some customer goals to shoot for might include

- Growing your total number of customers
- Obtaining new customers
- Growing the purchases made by existing customers
- Retaining customers
- Improving customer satisfaction ratings (based on customer satisfaction research)
- Obtaining specific customers (such as important influencers or major corporations)
- Setting up additional distribution channels to reach new customers
- Amassing a certain number of customer testimonials
- Creating a customer database

Bright Idea

For more help in setting and tracking your progress toward your goals, try out www.MyGoals.com. You can try the service free for ten days or sign up for $5.95 per month, for as long as you'd like support. You can also read articles about goal setting there, or skim tips to become more skilled at setting realistic goals.

Especially in a company's early years, attracting and retaining customers should account for a significant portion of marketing goal setting. Those satisfied early customers can form a devoted base that will help attract other customers.

Image goals

In addition to financial and customer growth and retention goals, image and branding goals are also important. In order for your business to grow and succeed, your customers need to perceive your company as best for meeting their needs. This is where marketing is key.

Your job is to convince as many people or companies in your target market that your business is the best choice for them. As word spreads, your customer base should expand, and the amount of business they do with you should increase. But creating a particular image for your business takes work, and some of your marketing goals should relate to how you want customers to perceive the company. When and how do you want them to think of your business? Should your business come up when a homeowner needs a low-cost solution? Or would you rather be known for charging a reasonable fee and providing unparalleled service?

Knowing how you want to be perceived is your goal, which marketing methods can then help you achieve. Some image-related goals that may apply to your business include the following:

- What one word should come to mind when customers hear your company name?

- Are you looking to overshadow a competitor this year, in the hopes of winning some of its business?

- Are you trying to evolve your company's image from one impression to a different one, such as from upscale to more affordable?

- Who are your desired customers (not to be confused with your existing customers, who may not fit where you want your business to move, image-wise)?

- Are you contemplating moving your business to better serve your clientele? Relocating into commercial space, into a class-A office building, or into a funky downtown loft all suggest different corporate images.

Marketing goals regarding your business image should reflect what you want your company's image and brand reputation to be in the future, based on how you intend to grow and expand it.

Just the facts

- A goal is a statement that describes a desired future situation, such as "Number one on the *Inc.* 500 list," or "Reach $5 million in sales within 24 months." After you've stated your objective (that is, your goal), you can then work backward to determine what actions will get you there.

- An effective goal is one that is positive, precise, performance-focused, realistic, prioritized, written down, scheduled, and challenging.

- Marketing goals generally address finances, customers, and/or the company image. A marketing plan is then drafted to determine how best to meet those goals.

GET THE SCOOP ON...
Understanding the benefits of planning ▪
Creating an effective marketing plan ▪
Setting a realistic budget ▪ Putting your
plan into effect ▪ Staying on track

Your Marketing Plan

Chapter 6

After you've studied your target market, identified your competition, and decided how to best position your company for business, it's time to create a formal marketing plan to put all that information to use. Until you commit your thoughts and ideas to paper, your marketing plan is little more than a wish, a goal, or a dream. But after you get those ideas down, your goals become more real and more achievable, and you can proceed to work on other aspects of managing your business. Writing down your plan releases your mind from having to constantly worry about all your activities. After it's on paper, your brain can relax a little.

Some business owners become edgy or nervous when they hear the word "plan," thinking that it's going to be too difficult or take too much time to prepare. If you happen to share that assumption, you'll be relieved to know that the marketing plan you'll start in this chapter won't cause pain or take weeks to complete. Granted, you can choose to spend as much time as you want on it—whether that means a few days or a few months—but you don't have to.

Using the format I discuss in this chapter, the plan won't take long, and you'll find that having a plan—a roadmap, if you will—in front of you will reduce the amount of time you spend thinking about marketing. Instead of evaluating different marketing opportunities that come up every week, you'll be able to refer to your marketing plan to see whether the new proposal, such as for a bigger phone book ad or 1,000 leather-bound notepads to give away at a trade show, makes sense for you and fits within your budget. Your marketing plan will guide those decisions to a large degree.

Why plan?

Why plan? In a nutshell, "if you fail to plan, you plan to fail." You may have heard that saying too many times already, but it's good advice. Rather than running your business on a day-to-day, crisis-by-crisis basis, if you invest some time thinking about what you want your company to be like, you'll spend far less time dealing with marketing problems later. A few hours spent looking ahead and strategizing the best use of your marketing dollars will yield far better results and require much less time to execute than working without a plan.

Another reason to write a marketing plan is to efficiently make decisions. Nothing gets in the way of progress more than indecision and waffling. If you have to evaluate every single new advertising or publicity or direct mail opportunity that comes along, you'll waste valuable time and end up with a marketing campaign that isn't well thought out.

That's not to say that you wouldn't be able to pull off very successful programs, such as creating a profitable Web site or devising a sales promotion that brings customers back again and again, but unless you have a marketing plan that pulls all your marketing activities together, you'll be missing opportunities to integrate them, which wastes money in the long run.

Bright Idea

For a free, fill-in-the-blanks marketing plan template provided by the Small Business Administration, go to www.sba.gov, click on Marketing, and click on Marketing Plans.

Integrated marketing, or a marketing approach that uses one marketing method to build on another, helps wring as much value as possible out of each method, while increasing the frequency with which potential customers hear about you. For example, a radio advertising campaign can make buyers aware of your company, just as an e-zine can. But by linking them together, such as by using the radio ads to encourage listeners to go to your Web site to sign up for the e-zine or by announcing the radio campaign in your e-zine and including the opportunity to win a prize by listening (which you arrange through your radio ad rep), you can get even better results.

Before you get into the nitty-gritty details of writing a plan (see the following section), keep in mind the general goals of the plan:

- To determine the total potential market for your products or services
- To identify your competitive advantage
- To define the various market segments of buyers within your target audience
- To describe how you will create demand for your products or services
- To state the strategies you'll use to generate and support demand
- To explain how you'll make the best use of your marketing budget

Outline of a plan

There are a number of different ways to prepare a marketing plan, but in this section, I fall back on the format taught at some of the top MBA programs. Using this approach, you'll end up with a plan that is comprehensive and that contains all your marketing information in one place, which will make finding important statistics and details easier later.

Executive summary

The first section of your marketing plan, the *executive summary,* is a summary that describes your business, what products or services you offer, who your target market is, and what your marketing goals are, such as opening another location, targeting a new market segment, or expanding geographically.

The executive summary need only be a few sentences long but is important if you intend to share your plan with anyone, such as your advisors, managers, or employees. Telling them up front what your current situation is and what you want to achieve with your marketing efforts in the coming year is helpful as they begin to read the specifics in later pages.

The executive summary can also be useful for you when you look back months or years from now to see how you approached your situation—it can remind you of your objectives without requiring you to read the entire document.

Some consultants advise also creating a mission statement that succinctly encapsulates all you're trying to do for customers, but I see it as optional. A mission statement can help solidify your goals and strategies, but it can also take quite a bit

---

 Watch Out!

Don't worry as much about format and presentation as you do about information flow and thoroughness. The information you include in your marketing plan is much more important than what it looks like on the page.

of time. You may want to put it on an action list for later, after the first draft of your plan is complete.

The challenge

The next section of your plan is your *challenge:* a short summary of what you want your marketing to achieve for you. Some possible objectives could include

- Market expansion
- Expansion into new target markets
- Introduction of new product lines
- Introduction of new services
- Overcoming competitive challenges
- Price increases
- Alignment with collaborators or partners
- New sales channels

These are only a few possibilities, but it's likely that your situation is somewhere within the preceding list.

To complete this section, write down what it is you hope your marketing program will achieve for your business—what is the challenge you're facing. Include sales figures or growth percentages you hope to hit in the next 12 months, as well as any other changes that will need to occur in order to reach your goal, such as adding staff or acquiring another company.

This section can run anywhere from a few paragraphs to a page or two, but don't let it go longer than two pages.

Situation analysis

In the *situation analysis,* you get much more detailed about your company and its market. This section helps you see, later on, which marketing techniques will yield the best results.

The main parts of this section of the plan address your company; your customers; your competition; the climate in which you're operating; and your strengths, weaknesses, opportunities, and threats, which is called a *SWOT analysis.* The purpose is to assess where you stand now so that you can plot a strategy that gets you where you want to be.

Company

In trying to decide where you're headed, it's a good idea to evaluate what's going on with your business right now. In other words, where do you stand? Some questions to think about, and to answer in writing, include the following:

- What are your short-term and long-term goals for your business?

- What are your current product and service offerings?

- How strong is brand awareness of your company?

- Why do most customers continue to do business with you?

- Are your current employees the best choices to support your company?

- Are you contemplating any joint ventures or alliances?

- What have your sales been? What percentage growth have you witnessed in recent years? To what do you attribute that growth?

In addition, make note of anything that makes your business stand out. When you review this section after you've written it, you should take away a solid understanding of what your business looks like and where it's headed.

Customers

After creating an overview of your company, you next want to focus on your *customer base,* to summarize who your customers

 Bright Idea

If you'd like to write a mission statement to further clarify what your business does and how it benefits your customers, take a look at the following article, which has a few examples of effective mission statements: www.businessplans.org/Mission.html.

are, how many there are, and why they choose to do business with you instead of your competitors. Some questions to answer include the following:

- Who are your core customers? How would you describe them demographically?

- In which market segments do you have the strongest following?

- What percent of your customers are returnees, and what percent are new?

- Where do you anticipate the strongest growth in the next couple of years? within these segments, or in new ones you aren't yet targeting?

- What are the key criteria that drive customers' decisions to purchase from you?

- Do certain customers buy particular types of products or brands? Or do they retain you for specific services?

The information in this section should provide a snapshot of your customers: why they buy from you and where the opportunities for growth lie.

Competition

The *competition* section of the situation analysis takes a look at your competitors. Be sure to refer to the competitor research you've already done to help complete this section. Some questions to answer here include the following:

- How many competitors do you have?

- Who are they, where are they, and how much of the market do they control?

- How do they differ from your company? How do their products, services, prices, and service compare, for example?

- What are their target markets? How do those markets match up with yours?

- Are there barriers to entry that would prevent new competitors from entering the market? (A *barrier to entry* is anything that could deter a new business from opening up, such as start-up costs, legislation, or existing competitors.)

- How are your competitors faring? Are sales increasing, or are some companies struggling?

- Has the market shifted in some way to cause such a change?

- What is the reputation of each competitor? How do those reputations compare to yours?

Feel free to address other points about your competitors that aren't mentioned on this list, too. This is a general guideline to help you assess how you can overcome any competitive pressures, and to identify specifically any opportunities you may have to win their business.

This section can be as short as a few paragraphs or as long as a few pages, depending on your market and whether competition is impacting your business's sales.

Climate

The *business climate* in which you're operating is affected by a number of external factors, such as politics, the economy, social and cultural trends, shifting demographics, and technology. Some of these factors will have a greater impact on your type of business than others, but you may find that one is a particularly strong influence. This section, which need not be long, identifies these five areas and describes any changes there that could create opportunities or damage your business's viability. Some of the information you might address include the following.

- **Politics:** Is there legislation or are there political movements that may increase your costs of operation or make it more difficult to stay afloat? Or could pending legislation remove some of the barriers you've been facing, or open up new customer segments?

- **The economy:** The state of the economy, and how positive consumers feel about it, can significantly impact your prospects for growth. If shoppers are nervous about rising inflation or major corporate layoffs, your marketing strategy may be quite different than if business everywhere is booming and consumers are making money hand over fist. What is the economic situation right now?

- **Social and cultural trends:** Although social movements and cultural trends generally occur over the long term, rather than in a few days or weeks, if you've noticed a consumer shift that spells good news or bad for your business, jot it down.

- **Shifting demographics:** What kinds of demographic changes are occurring that might spell opportunity or danger for your industry? What age group currently accounts for the largest percentage of consumers in your area—or nationwide? Which age group is experiencing the greatest growth? Who is likely to be buying from you in the coming years?

- **Technology:** Are there technological changes, products, or trends that could affect how you do business in the next few years? Is your company currently investing in new technology to avert a problem down the line? How are you making the most of technology, while avoiding any potential pitfalls it may cause?

As a business owner, there are certainly areas of your company you can control—what you pay your employees, what your hours of operation are, how many networking events you'll attend this month. But there are also things you can't control, most of which are cited in the preceding list.

Because you have no control over external factors, it is important to identify them and develop strategies for taking advantage of them or mitigating any damage they can do to your bottom line. Marketing can help with both issues.

Watch Out!

Don't use a weak economy as an excuse for why your company's sales may be down. People and companies are still buying, even in a recession. Ignore what you hear about the state of the economy, which you can't impact, and focus instead on what you can do to create business opportunities for your company. Success is certainly possible, even during tough times.

SWOT analysis

Another way to look at the environment in which you're doing business is through a SWOT analysis, so named because it addresses your company's Strengths and Weaknesses, over which you have some degree of control, as well as your Opportunities and Threats, which are less within your control.

Your *strengths* are aspects of your company or its products and services that customers approve of and appreciate. They are the reasons, or contributors to, why people do business with you. Your strengths could be anything from your physical location to the expertise of your senior managers to your guaranteed level of service. Market share, sales growth, and a technological lead are other examples of strengths, the results of which cause your competition to have a hard time catching up to you.

Your business's *weaknesses* are areas where you could use some improvement. They're your competitive disadvantages, which might be a bad reputation, limited product selection, or lack of adequate distribution channels. Anything that gets in the way of or dissuades customers from doing business with you are weaknesses. And it's important to lay them all out in writing in your marketing plan so that you can begin to strategize how to reduce or eradicate them.

Opportunities, on the other hand, are the possibilities for future business, based on events in the marketplace. They emerge due to changes in the external marketplace, rather than due to some marketing strategy you may come up with, and have the potential to seriously change your company. They are the possible home runs that you'll want to keep your eye on so that you can position yourself to take advantage of every one, whether it's a current competitor that is considering getting out of the business and is looking for a buyer, or a new law or new technology that will render other businesses obsolete. These are all potential opportunities for your business.

Conversely, *threats* are possible downturns in your business due to external events over which you have little or no control. Events such as a looming transit strike, or a potential shortage in an important raw material because of an overseas plant fire, would qualify as threats to your business. And because you have little control over them, all you can do is prepare how you can best respond and react to them, in the hopes of lessening the damage they may cause.

A SWOT analysis is fairly brief, can be structured as a series of bulleted paragraphs, and runs anywhere from one to three pages.

Market segmentation

The *market segmentation* section is the area of your plan where you should talk about the various customer segments you sell to, or intend to sell to. Some companies have very detailed segments with some overlap depending on age or lifestyle, while other businesses may only have two or three. There is no right answer here—it all depends on who you're trying to appeal to.

 Bright Idea

Sometimes getting an objective assessment of your company can be immensely helpful when conducting a SWOT analysis. If you have an advisory board, tap it for insight into your strengths, weaknesses, opportunities, and threats. Or pull together a group of customers, suppliers, and advisors to get their input. Your evaluation will likely be much more complete and accurate with their help.

For each segment, provide a brief overview, perhaps with a short name to identify it, such as the Small Business Stars or Extreme Sports Fanatics. In addition, you'll want to briefly describe the characteristics of each segment, preferably using bullet points for ease of reading. Key descriptors to address are as follows:

- Name and brief description

- Demographics: age, education level, household size, and so on

- Purchase trigger: why, when, and how they use your products or services

- Frequency of use

- Preferred means of information gathering: print, telephone, Internet, referrals from friends, and the like

- Price sensitivity

- What percent of sales they account for at your company (the total for all of your segments should equal 100 percent)

Marketing strategy

How you decide to market your company and its products and services should be based on the *four Ps*—product, price, place, and promotion.

Product

Your marketing strategy—how you will convince customers to buy from you—is based in large part on the products and services you provide. Any competitive advantages you can leverage help shape your marketing message and woo buyers. In particular, evaluate the following about your products and/or services:

- **Quality:** How does it stack up against the competition? Is it better or worse than what customers expected? What do customer satisfaction surveys indicate? You discover more about surveys in Chapter 18.

- **Brand:** Are your products and services sold under a particular brand name that prospects recognize and respond positively to? Is the brand an advantage or disadvantage in selling?

- **Level of expertise:** In services, are your workers adequately trained to tackle the most common customer challenges? Are they able to identify and provide the services the customer requested in a timely manner?

- **Breadth:** How comprehensive is your product line or your service capabilities? Do your customers generally have to supplement their purchases from you with offerings from another company? Or is your selection second to none?

- **Technical support:** When customers buy from you, are they happy with the level of support that accompanies their purchase? Is any support they might need readily available? Is it free? Does it meet their needs?

- **Guarantee:** Does your company stand behind its wares and services, offering some kind of assurance that customers will get what they expect from you?

Price

How you price your products and services has a major impact on sales. Price them too high, and the size of your potential customer base shrinks, although you may also attract customers who prefer exclusive brands. Price them too low, and you'll have lower profits while potentially wearing your staff out, either from providing services or keeping up with demand for your products. Finding the happy medium, where you have enough demand to keep everyone busy while still being profitable, without overtaxing your resources, is tricky. Sometimes it even takes some testing to determine what price yields the best results.

In your marketing plan, you'll want to explain the following in relation to your pricing:

- How do you determine your prices? Do you mark up the wholesale cost by a set percentage? Do you charge what everyone else charges per hour for your services? What's your strategy?

- What are your basic costs? What profit margin are you assuming or are you aiming for?

- Will you offer customers payment terms? What will they be?

- Have you arranged for outside financing to help customers afford your products and services?

- In what instances, if any, will you give volume discounts?

In most cases, pricing is a fluid process. You may start at one price and adjust it as you see how customers respond to it. But by putting your rationale on paper, you'll have an easier time keeping track of which pricing approaches work best.

Place

Where you distribute your products and services—and how—is tackled here. In addition to considering various locations that might best suit your company, you also need to weigh your distribution options, such as retail, online, direct to consumer, manufacturer's reps, and agents. Finally, you'll want to explain any logistical strategy, if applicable, such as whether you sell products that need to be shipped, transported, or warehoused.

 Watch Out!

Managing your distribution channels can be tricky, especially when there is overlap. Allowing retailers to sell online, for example, sets up a potential clash over territory. Or allowing several agents to represent your work may lead to squabbles over where your allegiance lies, and who gets credit for a sale. To avoid disagreements, most companies try to keep their distribution channels totally separate.

Promotion

All the preceding information leads to decisions about which marketing methods make the most sense for your company. Although you hear so much more about each of these tactics in Parts III, IV, and V, be aware that in this section, you explain which methods you'll use, how they'll support each other, and how you'll allocate the available funds across all your initiatives.

The main promotional methods you'll be considering include the following:

- Advertising
- Public relations
- Telemarketing
- Networking
- Sales promotion
- Public speaking
- Image building
- In-person marketing
- The Internet
- Marketing literature

Sales projections

Of course, the whole point of marketing is to generate sales and create new business opportunities, which you estimate using sales projections. *Sales projections* are your best guess at what your company will sell in total in the coming month, quarter, and year. By tracking the results from each individual marketing program, whether it is telemarketing calls or public speeches, you'll be better able to link those activities to specific contracts or customers. And you'll have a better handle on which are worth continuing in the future. Setting up your monthly sales projections is easiest if done in a spreadsheet program, such as Excel, which can be updated and modified as the year progresses.

Bright Idea

If you'd like to see what financial projections should look like, check out the sample financial statements at www.bplans.com/spv/3383/4.cfm#1040000. Keep in mind that the complexity of your financial projects should match the stage and size of your company. A start-up's financials will be much less complicated, while a multi-million dollar venture may be more so. Use these samples as a general guide.

Estimate annual sales

At the start of your marketing plan, without past sales figures, you'll need to estimate your annual sales. Breaking them down by month is helpful so that you can compare them to the months when you had the most marketing activities. And if you have past sales figures, you can easily adjust them to reflect the amount of business you expect to do in the coming year.

Set the dreaded budget

Setting a marketing spending limit is tough, especially after you take a close look at all the wonderful promotional opportunities out there. Yes, there are a million ways to spend your marketing dollars, and the trick is setting a budget that is reasonable for your company's size, stage of development, and industry.

The general guideline for marketing spending at established companies is around 4 percent of gross sales. That means that for every $100,000 your company earns in revenue, you should be investing about $4,000 of it in marketing. So if you take 4 percent of your company's total sales, you have a rough estimate of what you should set aside for your marketing activities in the next 12 months.

However, companies that are more mature, with an established client base, are generally going to spend less on marketing than a start-up that is in full-blown growth mode. A business with no name recognition and a small but growing client base is going to need to spend more to be competitive. Newer companies

Bright Idea

Many trade associations track the performance of their participants—anonymously, of course—in order to provide members with a tool for comparison and tracking. Check with your industry's association to learn whether they may have statistics they can share to help you assess how your company stacks up.

spend, on average, about 10 percent of sales during the early years, and then reduce it, as needed.

That's not to say that you *must* reduce your spending, but that some companies elect to over time. You'll also want to keep in mind that if your competition routinely spends 4 or 5 percent of sales on marketing and you decide to invest 6, 7, or 8 percent, you have the potential to make significant advances in obtaining more market share. Maintaining your higher level of marketing spending could give you a sizeable competitive advantage.

Another factor in setting your marketing budget is the industry in which you're working. There are standard percentages for most industries, just as each industry has its own typical marketing methods. And you may find that your industry, perhaps because it is new or because it has recently been hit with negative press, must spend more than other types of businesses in order to attract customers. Investigate what most businesses in your industry of a similar size are spending, percentage-wise, on their marketing.

A marketing plan's long-term value

A marketing plan has historical value in that it can serve as a record of where you've been, what you've tried that worked, what you've tried that didn't work, how you responded to competitors and external challenges, and how the company has grown. Unless you write it down and preserve it, you'll likely have trouble remembering how much you spent on your last brochure, for example, or why in the world you elected to fly to

London for an industry trade show. But if you make note of it in your plan, you'll always be able to look back and learn from your experience.

And the biggest value of a plan is in its role as a reference tool. After you've written everything down, you'll want to pull it out regularly—or even tack key pages on your bulletin board, where you'll see them every day—to ensure that every decision you make supports your long-term goals and objectives.

Just the facts

- A marketing plan is beneficial for a number of reasons, including saving time and money, as well as improving the overall effectiveness of marketing tools in use.

- The physical act of writing down your intentions increases the odds that they will come to fruition. And having your plans and ideas down on paper makes it much easier to discuss them with others and refer back to them.

- Rather than dealing with marketing initiatives on a case-by-case basis, making long-term plans can yield better pricing because you're buying in larger quantities. This is true whether you're dealing with advertising, giveaways, travel, or printing. Knowing what you're going to need for the next 12 months provides a significant opportunity to negotiate better pricing from suppliers.

- The basic sections of a marketing plan are the executive summary, challenge, situation analysis, market segmentation, marketing strategies, and projections.

- Although companies use a variety of methods to determine how much to spend on marketing each year, the general guideline is 4 percent of sales. However, newer companies should spend as much as 10 percent (more, if they can) to raise overall awareness for their products, services, and brand name.

The Least Expensive Ways to Market Your Business

GET THE SCOOP ON...
Making your company newsworthy ▪ Finding
media opportunities ▪ Disseminating information
effectively ▪ Getting the word out

PART III

Public Relations

P ublic relations happens to be one of the most effective ways of marketing your business. Surprisingly, it's also one of the least expensive. That gives you two big reasons to include plenty of public relations activities in your marketing plan.

Public relations activities involve informing the public about your company and its products and services, which helps to shape your reputation and image. In many cases, this information is communicated to the public via the media, including TV and radio stations, newspapers, magazines, newsletters, and news Web sites. This aspect of public relations is called *publicity,* and it should be the focus of your public relations activities.

The key to being successful with public relations comes down to three factors:

- Whether the information is relevant to the target media
- Whether it is sent to the proper person
- Whether it is in the format the media prefers for such information

Watch Out!

When creating public relations materials, be sure superlatives like "amazing," "revolutionary," or "best," which set off alarm bells in the minds of reporters and editors, are rare or nonexistent. Also, steer clear of a tone that is overly promotional and use a more objective or newsy style.

Relevancy

To determine whether the information you're sending out to your target audience is relevant, you need only ask one question: "Who would care about this?" Put another way, is the recipient likely to be interested in what you have to say?

For example, your local business newspaper is responsible for reporting news about the area's business community and will probably welcome hearing about your company. However, the same information is not relevant to business newspapers outside your area, where you have no connections.

Likewise, media in your industry are likely to be interested in hearing about your company, because you're a participant in their field. But media in other, unrelated, industries couldn't care less. For example, if you're a software developer, keep in touch with reporters in the software and computing fields, but sending information to media in the banking and pharmaceutical industries would be a waste of time—they don't report about software development.

To come up with a possible list of media to send public relations materials to, consider the following:

- Local publications and broadcast media
- State and regional media
- Alumni publications that your alma mater produces
- Industry publications
- Trade association media for organizations of which you're a member

Money Saver

A comprehensive resource to use in preparing a media list for your business is Bacon's Directories (www.bacons.com). It lists virtually every media, including contact information. The cost is around $300 per directory, but many advertising agencies and business libraries also have them.

- Professional association media for groups of which you're a member
- Civic organization media for organizations to which you belong
- Media for industries where your product or service is a good fit
- Web sites read by people in your field, including your target audience

After you've identified the media outlets most likely to be interested in hearing from you, the next step is to drill down and find the particular editor, producer, reporter, or writer who is your best point of contact at each newspaper, magazine, TV station, or radio station.

Contact point

Although many people do it, blindly addressing public relations materials to "Editor" or "Reporter" at a particular publication or station is a mistake. Failing to get a live person's name suggests you either don't know what you're doing or were too lazy to pick up the phone and ask to whom you should mail your information.

It's actually quite easy to ascertain the appropriate editor's name, phone number, and e-mail address. It's also an important step in getting your information into that person's hands.

After you have a broadcast station's name and address, you can easily do an online search to get the main phone number. The last step is to call and ask for the assignment editor's name. Or, if you're reluctant to pick up the phone, you can spend a

Bright Idea

To find out which stories reporters and editors are currently working on, for which they may need sources, consider subscribing to PR Leads (www.prleads. com). For around $100/month, you'll receive regular e-mails regarding stories for which you may be a great resource.

little more time searching online to see whether the person's name is listed somewhere on the station's Web site.

For national TV shows like *Oprah* or *The Today Show*, it's more difficult to determine the name of the right person to talk to. In this case, you'll be aiming to catch the attention of a producer, rather than an assignment editor. One strategy to gather the names of producers is to tape the tail end of the show and scroll slowly through the names of the producers listed. After you have some names, you can call and get some advice on the best producer to whom to pitch your idea.

The same process also works for newspapers and magazines, where the trick is getting the name of the editor who handles the section of the publication in which you want to be mentioned. As a small business, you clearly qualify for the business section, but depending on your offerings, you may also aspire to be covered in the personal finance section, the lifestyle section, or the sports section. Whatever your specialty, when you find out the name of the editor responsible for that section, you've significantly upped your chances of publicity in that publication.

PR tools

After zeroing in on the media outlets and individual contact names, your last challenge is preparing newsworthy information in the format that the editors and reporters prefer. There are a number of public relations tools to choose from, including press releases, press kits, pitch letters, articles, case studies, white papers, and photographs.

Press releases

Press releases are one or two-page, double-spaced documents that are best used to make a simple announcement, such as a new hire, a recent award, or the opening of additional locations, for example.

Press releases are fairly easy to write and easy to distribute, but because they are so plentiful they are also easily lost or misplaced after they land on an editor's desk. For that reason, they may not be the best choice for major announcements, such as a new-product release or details regarding a lawsuit settlement.

Sending a photo along with a press release has been shown to increase the odds that the information will be used. For mailed press releases, attach with a paper clip a photo of your expanded warehouse, the employee who was just promoted, or the huge trophy your company just won. If you're sending an electronic press release, however, ask before attaching an electronic image, because many publications refuse to open attachments. In addition, large images can jam e-mail servers.

For guidance in how to properly format a press release, check out www.marketingsource.com/pressrelease/releaseformat.html, where you'll find an easy-to-follow template you can use to write yours up.

Press kits

Major announcements are better served by a full-blown press kit than a single release. A *press kit* typically includes one or more press releases, some background materials, frequently asked questions, photos, and media contacts. These documents are

---

 Money Saver

Although you may have already compiled your own list of the media most appropriate for your particular company and announcement, consider sending any press release out nationwide using PRWeb, a free online press release distribution service, at www.prweb.com.

Bright Idea

Whenever you send out public relations materials to an editor, attach a short greeting expressing your appreciation for their time and willingness to consider including your information in an upcoming issue or show. Gratitude and humility will get you much further than arrogance or pushiness.

often neatly packaged in a two-pocket folder, with the company's logo emblazoned on the cover in some fashion, such as a printed label, sticker, or embossing device.

In addition to providing far more space to elaborate on a significant announcement, press kits also look much more substantial. Their appearance suggests that they contain meaty information, and their sheer size makes them stand out more among the piles of press releases lining an editor's desk.

The only real downsides of preparing a press kit are the time and money required. Because there may be several documents enclosed, more time will be needed to pull them together. And the cost of the paper, photos, pocket folders, and mailing the oversized package will be a good bit higher than sending out a simple two-page press release. But the amount of coverage you may earn could easily justify that expense.

Pitch letters

Where press releases and kits are used to try to persuade an editor to give publicity to your business, *pitch letters* are documents used to try to persuade an editor or producer to tackle a particular issue or topic. These one-page letters are sent to an individual editor and outline an idea you may have for a specific article or show, including mentioning how you may be of assistance in pulling it together. Perhaps you'd be a great resource, or maybe you can put the editor in touch with potential interviewees. Whatever your proposed role, mention that in the letter.

Being quoted in an article or interviewed on TV or radio gives you immediate credibility as an expert in your field. But sometimes, such opportunities won't arise until you help an editor come up with a story idea that would include you. That's where pitch letters are perfect.

Article submissions

If you have an idea for an article that you would like to write yourself, call or write the editor to inquire about opportunities for article submissions. Many trade journals accept articles written by members or outside experts, for example. The first step is merely to ask the editor if the publication accepts article submissions and, if yes, what the requirements are in terms of topics and word count (how long the article can be).

The advantage of submitting an article is that you can control 99 percent of what is in the article—the remaining 1 percent covers changes the editor will presumably make. In many cases, your name will be mentioned at the top of the article as the author, and some publications may even ask for a photo to run alongside it. Whenever possible, ask whether your contact information or your company's Web site can be mentioned at the end of the article, thus making it easy for potential customers to get in touch with you.

> 66 Studies at the Harvard Business School estimate that a news item that refers to your product, company, or service is worth ten times more than the advertising cost of that space or air time. That extra value—that additional credibility—is because of the implied editorial endorsement of the press. 99
>
> —Sandra Beckwith, author, *Streetwise Complete Publicity Plans*

Case studies

Another form of article, which trade journals especially love, is the case study, also called a success story. A *case study* is a type of article that describes how an individual or company benefited from using your company's product or service. Chapter 11 has additional details about case studies.

Watch Out!

When a reporter calls to follow up on information you've sent them, be aware that everything is on the record. If you're not prepared to talk right then, ask whether you can call them back in ten minutes. And then use that time to think through potential responses.

Case studies generally start with a description of the situation before the customer began working with you, and end with a description of how things have changed—a "before and after" scenario. Depending on space constraints, it is often useful to provide a little detail regarding how the transformation occurred.

In addition to trade journals, case studies are common on Web sites and in newsletters, so look for varied opportunities to submit them.

White papers

In fields like technology, government, and medicine, *white papers* are common communication tools, reporting on a particular issue, that often take a position, rather than remaining neutral. In general, white papers describe how the implementation of a particular product or technology provides a solution to a problem, often arguing for or against a particular strategy. They are also called position papers.

White papers can be quite lengthy, allowing plenty of space to make a case for the issue at hand. But those that are purely self-promotional, rather than educational, are not taken seriously.

For more information about white papers, and how to write one, check out the following Web site: www.stelzner.com/copy-HowTo-whitepapers.php.

Photographs

Sometimes, a photograph is all that is needed to tell a story, or to highlight something of potential interest to an editor. When coupled with a short caption describing what the image shows, some photos have been known to be used as standalone stories in newspapers and magazines.

Send out relevant and interesting photos to editors much like you would a press release, with a label on the back explaining the photo.

More advanced PR tools

Small businesses that use even a few of these tools, or document formats, will often see their public visibility soar, and their reputation spread quickly. Success breeds success, especially where the media is concerned, and one mention in the newspaper can generate corresponding interest on the part of other papers, magazines, and TV and radio producers.

After you become accustomed to regularly distributing information about your company using press releases, press kits, articles, case studies, white papers, and photos, you may decide to try to leverage that success to get into the big leagues. For some companies, that means national exposure, for others, it means a regular spot on local TV or radio. Either way, there are a number of public relations targets to shoot for.

Writing a column

If you've been regularly submitting articles to certain trade journals or the local paper, you may want to explore the idea of writing a column. The benefit of a column is that you earn ongoing publicity, including perhaps a small photo and byline next to your article. The only challenge is making sure you have enough material to keep you going for months or years on end.

 Bright Idea

If you're convinced that writing a book will do wonders for your business, but don't have the time to create it yourself, consider hiring a ghostwriter to do the work for you. Many well-known public figures have relied on a professional writer to help get their books into production.

If you've published several articles already and have ideas for many more on a particular subject, you're in a good position to propose a regular column. To do so, write a letter to the editor of the publication in which you'd like to be featured, and include clips from previously published articles and a list of potential future topics you could tackle. If you can come up with a clever or catchy title for your column, so much the better.

Keep in mind the ultimate objective of your writing the column, which is to heighten awareness of your company. With that in mind, in order to get the biggest payback from your efforts, you'll want to propose a column that speaks to your target audience. If you're a restaurateur, your column could be all about healthy eating or trends in food. The owner of a clothing store could regularly write about fashion trends, finding clothes that fit, or profiling fashion designers. Keeping the information useful and reflecting positively on your business is important, so stay away from controversial topics at all cost.

Sure, you could propose a column on your hobby or pet interests, but instead of helping to further your business goals, such a commitment would surely take time away from your business.

Authoring a book

Another credibility-building tool for small business owners, especially those in the service industry, is authoring a book. Being able to say that you're a published author lends an air of authority and prestige that few others can match.

However, because of the time and energy required to write a book, this tactic should be carefully evaluated before proceeding. Some businesses, such as consulting, speaking, interior decorating, financial management, and other service specialties, lend themselves to selling a book better than others.

Writing a book puts such professionals on a higher tier than their competitors, as well as providing an additional revenue stream. But many small businesses, such as tool and die shops, engineering firms, and computer repair dealers, will not benefit as much from publishing a book.

Watch Out!

Press conferences may look like an efficient way to make a big announcement to all the media, but rarely are they worth the effort. You're at the mercy of TV, radio, and newspaper crews, who may not even show up if a more exciting news story occurs.

Speaking in public

I go into much more detail on this topic in Chapter 9, but accepting opportunities to speak in front of members of your target audience is another smart public relations tactic. Of course, many people absolutely hate public speaking, so that limits this option. But if you enjoy chatting about topics near and dear to your heart, speaking engagements are a great way to position you as the expert.

When you're up front at the podium, you're the leader—the person who knows more than just about everyone in the room—and such opportunities reinforce the notion that you're a savvy business person.

There are so many opportunities to speak for free, however, that you want to limit your appearances to those made to an audience of potential customers or referral sources. And the topic should somehow relate to your business; otherwise, you'll spend hours preparing a talk that won't ultimately aid your marketing efforts.

Getting on the radio

Although a big focus of this chapter is on print media, simply because there are more opportunities there than in broadcast, landing a radio or TV interview is not impossible. In fact, sometimes broadcast media has a broader reach than publications in print and can help publicize your business even better than a newspaper or magazine.

If you believe you have the talent and personality for radio, you may decide to pursue broadcast publicity through radio interviews. In fact, radio interview opportunities are frequent and plentiful, because you can conduct phone interviews that are broadcast live on radio stations almost anywhere, from the comfort of your office or home. Borrowing or buying a guide to radio stations can help you scope out your best opportunities for media coverage, either locally, regionally, or nationally.

And if you find you really like radio, you may want to explore hosting a regular radio show. Such opportunities are generally available only on smaller stations or on local talk networks, but if you can outline a program different from what's currently on the market, and that would be of interest to the station's listeners, you may have your proposal seriously considered.

Of course, the more radio experience you've had, the better your case, but a lack of experience won't necessarily nix your chances.

Develop your proposal by describing what kind of show you'd like to host, how frequently, for what length of time, and what kinds of topics you would cover. Then present it to the station manager for consideration.

Getting your company on TV

If your business is visual, or there are opportunities to show you in action, television coverage may be an excellent marketing tool. Local TV stations are constantly on the look out for a good story, especially if there is something that can be captured on camera. For example, if you are a professional organizer, perhaps you could be filmed helping a viewer organize his or her home. Or if you run a summer camp, there must be regular opportunities to showcase your staff in action during the summer months.

Think of events that are coming up that might be appropriate for a local station to show on-air, and then send an e-mail or a letter to the news editor or assignment editor at the station.

Although many business owners would love to host their own show, rather than being interviewed on one, convincing a television station to give you control of one of their time slots will be nearly impossible, unless you start with a local public access channel.

Public access channels, which are often run by volunteers, have time to fill and may be willing to give you a regular time slot to fill, as long as your material will be of potential interest to local viewers.

Beyond publicity

Although publicity is an extremely cost-effective way to market your business, there are other public relations tactics that can be useful as well. The common theme is communicating with your target audience, which should include your customers, potential customers, suppliers, the media, and sources of referral. Keeping them abreast of your business's accomplishments, milestones, and news encourages them to tell others of your success.

Newsletters

Newsletters, handy communiqués that are sent out regularly to customers or employees, are another proven public relations tool. Although many newsletters today are sent out electronically, at minimal cost, print newsletters work just as well at letting your customers know what you've been up to.

With newsletters, it's important to commit to a regular schedule so that recipients can start to anticipate them; sending them whenever you feel like it doesn't help keep your company's name top-of-mind and suggests you're not very organized. Consider starting with a quarterly schedule (four times per year), and then increase to bi-monthly or monthly after you get the hang of it. It's better to increase the frequency after you

 Bright Idea

Elaine Floyd's book *Marketing with Newsletters* is an excellent resource for companies in the process of creating a new internal or external newsletter.

Money Saver

Plan ahead and produce two issues of your newsletter at once to save production costs. Fees for layout, writing, and printing of two issues together will all be significantly less than for two separate ones.

know it's worth the time and money than to start at a monthly frequency and scale back later.

Interestingly, the length of the newsletter doesn't seem to have much impact on the effectiveness, so why not just start with a two-page issue—the front and back of an 8.5" x 11" sheet of paper. If you discover you always have more to say, you can switch to an 8.5" x 17" ledger size sheet and fold it in half to make a four-page newsletter.

For all the dirt on newsletters, check out Chapter 11.

Corporate Web site

Although many public relations tactics involve distributing information to potential clients and constituents, making information available for people who are looking for it is equally important. This is where a Web site can come in handy.

As more consumers and businesses have come to rely on the Internet as a communications device and information resource, having a company Web site has become even more important.

When a potential customer has a need for your company's products or services or wants to learn more about what you do, a Web site is an excellent passive source of that information. By designing a Web site and making it available to anyone on the Internet, your Web site is working for you 24 hours a day, answering questions and providing information to anyone who stops by. You don't have to interact with each customer, as a phone call would require, nor do you even have to be awake. Your Web site is up and running even when you aren't.

The primary purpose of a Web site is to provide the public with information. Some companies elect to build in e-commerce capabilities that allow visitors to make a purchase, but the time and money required to do so may not be worthwhile for you. More important, your Web site can reinforce the company image you want to project and encourage potential customers to buy from you.

See Chapter 10 for much greater detail on online marketing.

Promotional products

Promotional products are those gadgets and giveaways featuring a company's name or logo—everything from sticky-back notes to rulers, pens and pencils, tote bags, mugs, and paper weights. They are public relations tools because they remind recipients of your company's existence and help shape their opinions of the business.

Many companies have giveaways created for certain events, such as a grand opening, open house, trade show, training session, or holiday party, so that attendees walk away with a little gift for their participation.

Promotional products do not have to be expensive to be effective, but they should have something to do with your business. For example, if you're a paint store, giving away something to do with painting or decorating would make sense—a small brush with your company's name and number on the handle, a drop cloth with your logo in the corner, or a handy carrier for paint chips would all be logical choices. The giveaway reinforces your business name and what you offer.

Personally, I like sticky-back notes because they work twice: The person who receives the package of stickies will find them handy, and each time a note is attached to a document, the original company's name is communicated to yet another person.

Don't waste your money on giveaways just for the sake of having something with your company name on it—it may backfire. I recall one financial services company that gave away clear rubber balls that lit up in the center when they hit the floor—cute toys, but what that had to do with finances of any kind, I don't know.

But general promotional products can work: Some sales people use candy jars as their giveaway. Then, whenever they're in the neighborhood, they stop by to refill the jar with some type of sweet. The point of any giveaway is to make the recipient feel positive about your company and to remind them of your avail-ability. There are hundreds of ways to do that, and your chal-lenge is to find a product that does that well within your budget. Skim the wide range of products at www.epromos.com for help in choosing a giveaway that's right for your business.

You'll find even more information about promotional prod-ucts in Chapter 15.

Just the facts

- Public relations is one of the most effective yet least expensive marketing methods available.

- Publicity is a subset of public relations, and it involves per-suading the media to give your company coverage.

- The secret to getting publicity is threefold: send relevant information to the right person in the format he or she prefers.

- In addition to pursuing media coverage, public relations involves developing ways to communicate regularly with your target audience, such as with a print or electronic newsletter, by using promotional products, or through a radio or TV show.

- Additional public relations tactics include creating a cor-porate Web site and sending promotional products.

GET THE SCOOP ON...
Mining your network of colleagues ▪
Reviewing the do's and don'ts of effective
networking ▪ Determining the best ways
to cultivate referrals ▪ Finding business
networking groups on and offline

Networking

Chapter 8

"It's not what you know, it's who you know," aptly summarizes the importance of business networking. Even with a superior service or product, your business won't be successful unless you find people willing to buy from you. And a network of contacts, or people you know through various ties to your industry or community, can help tremendously in finding and selling potential customers. In many ways, your network of colleagues, associates, and customers is your marketing team.

Among other things, your network can help identify the appropriate person to contact at a company you want to do business with, can alert you to upcoming opportunities in a particular organization, can introduce you to potential clients, or, even better, can recommend you when the opportunity arises. Your network opens doors and often paves the way to new business opportunities, which is why networking should be a top priority in your marketing mix. In addition, it costs so little to do compared to other marketing methods, requiring only the cost of your business cards; the cost to attend luncheons, meetings, or special events; and the cost to travel to and from such gatherings. And ultimately, the best networkers are always meeting new people—not just during specific functions or events.

Be prepared

As with any type of marketing activity, you'll achieve much better results from your efforts if you take time to prepare before you begin.

Define who you'd like to meet

The first step is defining who you'd like to meet. You can state this in terms of a list of key individuals you'd like to meet who can connect you with other people who can aid your business, or as a general description of the type of person you want to get to know, such as chief financial officers (CFOs) at mid-sized companies, top sales reps, or busy moms of toddlers.

After you know who is in a position to help your business, assess where you're likely to find your best contacts. If you're looking for specific people, your search will be a little easier because you can zero in on what organizations they belong to, what charitable groups they're involved with, and any mutual acquaintances you have. With that information, you can ask for an introduction or make an effort to connect with them at an upcoming event. But if your current needs are more general, you'll want to think more broadly about where your target audience is spending time. Depending on their demographics, you may find them at a local health club, at local fundraisers, at board meetings, or at your child's school, for example.

Prepare an elevator speech

After you've created a general list of where your target audience can be found, prepare a short verbal presentation to quickly introduce yourself. Often called an *elevator speech* because it should be short enough that you can deliver it while traveling between floors on an elevator, this brief statement summarizes what you may be able to offer the person you're talking to. It should answer the question "Who are you and what do you do?" But if that's all you say, you won't make a very big impression.

To develop your elevator speech, try to answer the following questions in 30 seconds or less, in only two or three sentences:

- What's your name?
- What's your business name and what do you do?
- What niche do you serve, if any?
- How are you different from your competition?
- What benefit(s) do your clients derive from doing business with you?

For example, instead of introducing yourself as "Jim Stewart, I own the men's clothing store next door," try to explain why people buy from you. "I'm Jim Stewart, I've been dressing top executives in town for the past ten years at Executive Clothiers. In fact, some have told me they believe they've been promoted because they look so polished and pulled together."

The key difference is that you've just explained why someone should do business with you and what makes your business unique, as well as prestigious—local executives have chosen

Bright Idea

If you've identified someone you'd like to do business with or who could be a vital link to an important business contact, take a few minutes to learn more about him or her. Do a Google search at www.google.com and read about the person's background, accomplishments, and interests, so you'll be able to start the conversation talking about them. Who can resist talking about themselves?

your business over the competition. You imply that the person you're speaking with should consider buying from you, too.

Depending on the person you're speaking to, you may want to adapt your speech somewhat. In this case, if you were talking to a woman, you'd want to mention that you make suits for women. Try to make the information relevant to the other person. And then ask what he or she does.

Networking works only through an exchange of information—otherwise, you've merely introduced yourself and have no idea to whom you're speaking.

Trade and professional organizations

If you're looking to mix and mingle with people in your industry, people who frequently are excellent sources of information about upcoming opportunities, consider becoming more active in the trade or professional organization for your business. There are associations for practically every type of company, but if you're having trouble tracking down the best one for you, consult the *Encyclopedia of Associations* at your local library or do a Google search to find national groups with a local chapter.

For example, if you're a retailer, check into your area's merchant association or chamber of commerce to network with fellow retailers. If you're a marketing consultant, your city's chapter of the American Marketing Association may have some great contacts, while a local consulting organization may put

---

 Watch Out!

Networking expenses can quickly eat into your budget if you try to join every possible organization in your area. Don't. Instead of spending money to attend many different networking events, choose one or two organizations where you see the biggest potential to develop relationships with people there. Then attend those meetings consistently. Go for quality and build relationships, not the largest business card collection.

Money Saver

If you're relatively new to your field, check into associate memberships many associations and trade groups offer, which are generally discounted from the full rate. Most associate memberships offer the same benefits as the full membership, but at a lower cost. Take advantage of it while you can!

you in touch with fellow consultants interested in exchanging tips and ideas for expanding their businesses.

In addition to mixing with people like you who may have useful information to share, explore organizations that your target audience belongs to. If you're a financial planner, for example, in search of small businesses with lots of money, you may want to check out the local associations for high net-worth businesses, such as dry cleaners. If you sell copiers, an organization for executives may be a solid source of contacts for you.

Getting to know important people in your industry is easier when you're a member and active participant in your profession's trade organization.

Alumni groups

Organizations to which you belong by virtue of a past association, such as having attended a particular college or worked at a large corporation, are another networking outlet.

Colleges and universities

Another good group to belong to, if there is one in your area, is the alumni organization for any college or grad school you attended. Many times, loyal alums are willing and interested in networking with fellow alumnae. The larger the college or university you attended, the greater the chance your city will have an active alumnae group. But even if there isn't one—you can find out by calling your college—this could be a great opportunity to start one. In addition to identifying who else in your area attended the same university, you'll position yourself as a leader by helping to get it up and running.

The main difference between alumni groups and professional associations is the organization's focus—alumni gatherings are frequently social in nature, while trade and professional get-togethers are almost entirely business focused. You'll need to decide, based on your business and goals, which types of organizations will do you the most good, but a mix may help bring you in contact with a broader range of people, thereby extending your own network further.

Corporate employers

Even if you didn't complete college, you may still qualify for another type of alumni group—those of former corporate employees. Anyone who used to work for a particular corporation qualifies for membership in its alumni group, which typically meets on a regular basis and provides a built-in network for workers to stay in touch, meet other former employees, and share news and information that may benefit other alums.

To find an alumni group for your former employer, start with the following:

- www.google.com, which may list group and meeting information

- www.linkedin.com, which has hundreds of alumni groups

- www.ryze.com, which is much like LinkedIn, with information about former colleagues

- www.groups.yahoo.com, on which many groups set up listservs; check to see whether there's one already established for your group

Volunteer and civic organizations

Another useful type of group to join include the many volunteer, civic, and charitable organizations in your area, which put

Bright Idea

Business cards and the contact information they contain are essential for effective networking. But keeping track of everyone you've met, when, and how to reach them can be cumbersome. Fortunately, CardScan (www.cardscan. com) is a tool that can help you better manage all those cards by scanning and converting the information to digital and storing it in a searchable database. It costs between $150 and $225, depending on which version you buy.

you in touch with people you might not normally run into. In addition, by volunteering to lead a committee or take on a project or position, you'll become familiar to and with other members of the organization. And that doesn't even begin to cover the good deeds you'll be doing in your community!

In addition to nonprofit organizations you may support, such as the American Cancer Society, Juvenile Diabetes Association, or American Heart Association, there are thousands of deserving hospitals, museums, schools, music programs, homeless shelters, pet rescue organizations, and so on. There are also civic organizations primarily for business leaders—that's you!—such as Rotary, Kiwanis, and the Jaycees, to name a few, which effectively blend business and community service.

By choosing an organization that does good work in the community and has ties to a personal interest or health concern, you'll have the chance to make a positive difference and meet others who may appreciate the support you're giving. Although networking opportunities are the focus of this chapter, I talk in Chapter 15 about sponsorships, which is another way you can support needy charitable groups and foundations.

Private clubs

Where volunteering is part social activity, networking at private clubs, such as country clubs, golf clubs, and dinner clubs, is all social. That's why members join—to enjoy the club's amenities and to develop friendships with other members. Yet the people

Money Saver

Many golf and country clubs offer a social member level that provides access to the club's meeting and dining facilities, but limits use of the athletic areas and is priced at a much lower cost than a full membership. If your goal is to have a nice place to entertain existing and potential clients, investigate whether a less expensive social membership will meet your needs.

who are members are also likely to have business ties that may prove useful.

Although the tax deduction for private social club memberships was eliminated several years ago, you may find in your area that joining a club is well worth the expense. It all depends on who you'd like to have in your network and where they generally spend their time. If the bulk of your target referral sources, mentors, and collaborators are not club-goers, this may not be the best place to invest your money and your time. However, if golf is a popular pastime in your area or if you believe your lunch or dinner invitations may be accepted more frequently if they were held at a private establishment, look into it. Some small business owners find they can more easily meet and chat with potential clients who happen to also belong to their club—for some it has resulted in significant business.

Online networking

Almost the polar opposite of private social clubs, where face-to-face contact is the norm, online networking Web sites are where business owners and professionals meet and greet electronically. The first generation of such sites was purely social, but from those pioneers came business-focused Web sites designed to connect business people with others.

Most online networking sites work by requiring you to register and provide some background information on who you are as well as on your clients, colleagues, friends, and so on. You can also invite others to join your network, thereby expanding your circle of contacts.

Based on your online network, you may be granted access to others you're interested in meeting. For example, if you've been dying to get an appointment with someone in research and development at Dell Computers, you can search the database to see who in your network may be able to link you to such a contact. On some sites, you make a request for contact that goes through your network's many layers before the person on the other end, at Dell, receives it and decides whether he or she is willing to grant your request—which might be for a phone conversation, a meeting, or to ask a few questions via e-mail.

Online networks mimic face-to-face networking in that your desire for information gets communicated to others in your immediate network until someone with connections can give you access to what you're looking for. If you want to find out how to land an appointment with a Wal-Mart buyer, someone on one of the Web sites is sure to have the answer. If you're looking to hire a top salesperson, you can ask others in your network for candidate recommendations. And, if you want to verify a rumor that one of your largest competitors is about to file for bankruptcy, it's likely someone in your network can check into it for you.

Although they each work slightly differently, if you have business-to-business needs, the following online networking sites may well be worth your while to join:

- **Ryze:** www.ryze.com

- **Spoke:** www.spoke.com

 Bright Idea

An advisory board, which can consist of mentors, suppliers, consultants, and other knowledgeable individuals, is another useful networking organization that you can design yourself. If you choose members who are well connected, they can be helpful in steering you to new opportunities and making important introductions. Such boards have no decision-making authority but meet regularly to give the leader input.

- **LinkedIn:** www.linkedin.com

- **ZeroDegrees:** www.zerodegrees.com

- **Entremate:** www.entremate.com

Most have a free trial period to allow you to see how the site works and whether it will help you network with the type of people who can help your company.

Networking groups and tip clubs

The brick-and-mortar equivalent of online networking Web sites are networking groups and tip clubs, which are private groups that meet regularly for the sole purpose of providing business leads and information to other members. There is typically a cost to join such groups as well as an ongoing commitment to be active and attend a certain number of meetings per month or per year. Many require members to come to meetings with at least one piece of information to share or a lead to pass along to a fellow member.

Some of the better-known of such organizations include

- Business Network International (www.bni.org)

- Company of Friends (www.fastcompany.com/cof/index.jsp), affiliated with *Fast Company* magazine

- Le Tip (www.letip.com)

- Leads groups sponsored by chambers of commerce; search www.2chambers.com to find your local chamber of commerce

---

 Money Saver

Smart barter exchange members treat their trade credits like cash—meaning they spend them judiciously—frequently using them to pay for ongoing expenses, such as janitorial services, payroll processing, or advertising, for example, thereby freeing up cash that would normally have been spent on such services.

Barter exchanges

Consider becoming a member of a *barter network*, called an *exchange*. These organizations consist of hundreds or even thousands of member companies who agree to accept trade credits—a cash equivalent—in place of cash when doing business with each other. The exchange takes a commission for each transaction it facilitates. Credits earned can be spent with any of the other member companies.

Bartering is worthwhile for companies with high enough margins to make it profitable even with the required commission on each sale. Many companies find bartering an excellent way to find customers who might never have considered them in the cash world. Bartering can also be useful for selling off excess inventory or keeping employees and equipment busy. Some companies find barter relationships can lead to cash relationships, too.

To find a barter exchange in your area, contact either of the following industry organizations:

- National Association of Trade Exchanges (NATE; www. nate.org)
- International Reciprocal Trade Association (IRTA; www. irta.com)

Bartering today is a totally legitimate way to do business, with the IRS receiving a record of your transactions at year end, and can provide immediate access to a network of businesses and consumers.

 Watch Out!

Before cutting a check to join a barter exchange, confirm that it's a good fit with your business. Ask about the demand for your products or services to get a sense of how much business you might have access to through the network. And review the current list of members to be sure you can find ways to spend your trade credits after you've earned them.

Bright Idea

Be prepared when potential clients ask for references by having a selection of written testimonials at-hand. Get in the habit of asking clients for a brief note expressing their satisfaction with the work you did for them or the product they bought from you after you've finished a project with them. Then, with their permission, use those testimonials to decorate your walls and feature them on your Web site, in your newsletter, and in your brochure. You'll enhance your credibility with new contacts even before you've met.

Referrals

One of the basic benefits of networking is the referrals that can result. Referrals are valuable because a customer, potential partner, supplier, or vendor who comes recommended to you by someone else has often already decided to do business with you, or may be predisposed to work with you, even if they are currently considering other options. The equivalent of word-of-mouth marketing, referrals can't be bought, which is why they are priceless.

Referrals shorten the sales cycle, increase your odds of converting the individual into a customer or collaborator, and reduce the amount of energy you need to invest in marketing. Think about it. Referral sources—people who are so confident in your abilities or pleased with what they've bought from you that they are willing to put their own reputation on the line to suggest your company—are like gold. Encouraging others to refer customers your way should be high on your list of priorities because it is an efficient use of your time and money.

The most successful referral relationships are built on personal experience and trust—both on your part and the part of the person being referred. Your best strategy is to build confidence in your company and trust within your network. People who know and trust you and your business will feel perfectly comfortable suggesting that others do business with you because they have witnessed the quality of your product or your work.

From time to time it is also smart to ask for referrals out-right. Let your existing customers know that you would welcome their help in identifying other customers like them. In some cases, it's as easy as asking a manager in one department whether he or she can refer you to another manager in the same company. Or, if you're a retail store, schedule a bring-a-friend night, during which your customers and their friends receive a special discount for coming in. Some businesses even offer incentives for customer referrals, such as a free month's membership, a free service, or a special gift. Whatever it is, make sure your customers know that you welcome referrals.

How *not* to network

You've seen them—the overbearing, pushy salespeople who net-work by inserting themselves into conversations, forcing their business cards on you, and then moving on to someone else after a few minutes. Yes, they may distribute and collect a slew of business cards by the end of an evening, but it's likely their net-working attempts will fall flat. Why? Because they show little or no interest in really understanding the needs of those they spoke with. And they were more focused on taking—cards and information—than on giving.

Focus on relationship building

Rule number one in networking is focus more on relationship building and less on the gathering of business cards. Unless you take the time to really introduce yourself and learn about those around you, it's unlikely they'll be willing to receive your follow-up phone call, despite their having given you their business card the night before. Getting to know people takes time, and with time comes trust and a greater willingness to help you.

Give more than you get

Rule number two is be more willing to give than to receive ini-tially. Look for ways you can help those you come in contact with, no matter how small. And continue to keep an eye out for opportunities to be of service. The more you do to help others, the more willing others will be to step up and assist you when you ask for it. Don't start your new business relationship by asking for a favor; instead, offer one.

Ask questions

Rule number three is ask questions. Focus more on learning about other people, by asking questions about them, their jobs, their companies, and so on, than on telling them all about you. They really don't care about you, to be honest, especially when you've first met. So use your time to get to know them, and they'll be more interested in hearing about you later.

Go slowly

Rule number four is to go slowly. The day after you've met the head of a local nonprofit is not the time to call and ask him or her to give you all their accounting work. You've asked for too much too soon. Your objective may be to win all the organization's accounting work, but to be successful, you'll need to learn all you can about their operations and how your organization is a better fit than their current provider. You certainly didn't figure that out during your five minute introductory conversation.

A better strategy is to call a couple of days later and ask the nonprofit head out to lunch, to learn more about what he or she does and what the nonprofit's needs are.

Networking is a process, not a quick fix. It can do wonders for your business if you work on creating and expanding your

 Watch Out!

When speaking with others, make sure you don't give the impression that you're purely a taker. Instead, early in the conversation, focus on how you may be of service to the other person. Perhaps they're looking for recommendations for a top-notch trainer or for a good restaurant for a business lunch. Offer information, connections, leads—whatever it sounds like other person needs—and you'll up the odds of future contact and help from that person.

network of colleagues, acquaintances, partners, suppliers, friends, and clients, all of whom will likely be your best source of new clients.

Follow up or fail

No matter how great your first meeting, how positive your first telephone conversation, or how promising your initial discussion with a potential client or referral source, you'll get absolutely nowhere if you don't follow up. That means sending an e-mail, a note, or making a phone call a few days after your last contact to confirm what was discussed and to inquire about a next step or to deliver whatever you may have promised during that conversation.

Then follow up again, whether to pass along some information you spotted that you thought they might be interested in, to extend a lunch invitation, or to inquire about the status of your previous business discussions. Keep the communication alive by staying in touch, and your network—and business opportunities—will grow quickly.

Just the facts

- Although networking typically happens naturally as part of your everyday interactions with people, creating a plan that ensures you meet members of your target audience or potential referral sources can help to build your business.

- The value of your network of contacts is the doors it can open for you. Through your network, you may be able to land a meeting with a potential client, find a reliable supplier, verify a job candidate's claims, and hear about upcoming opportunities before your competition, among many possible benefits.

- One of the most important tools of networking is your elevator speech, which is a 30-second summary of who you are, what you do, and what benefits your customers derive from doing business with you. This explanation of your company's benefits is key and sets you apart.

- Identifying where your target audience is likely to spend time is one way to zero in on networking opportunities. For example, you'll likely have more luck running into senior executives at a private country club, civic organization meeting, health club, or community event than at work.

- There are also networking organizations, on and offline, established expressly to bring business to their members, including barter exchanges, which are another way to develop new customer relationships.

- Although it may feel like making the initial contact is the most important step in networking, following up and staying in touch is much more so. Many business relationships never go anywhere, and opportunities are lost because one or both of the parties didn't pursue them.

GET THE SCOOP ON...
Being the expert at the front of the room ■
Recognizing how teaching seminars opens door ■
Finding speaking opportunities ■ Getting
past your fear of speaking

Public Speaking

Chapter 9

Outside of public speaking, there are few situations where you are instantly perceived as the most knowledgeable person on a particular topic simply by standing in front of the room. Accepting the opportunity to speak about a topic with which you're familiar, or on which you have an opinion, to an audience of your prospects, fans, or potential referral sources is priceless—yet rarely is there a cost (and sometimes you're even paid a small fee). Public speaking provides exposure, credibility, and prestige all in one, if only you're willing to stand in front of a crowd and speak—and not everyone is.

When it comes to low-cost marketing methods, public speaking is right up there with public relations and networking in terms of solid results for little investment. Not only does speaking in public position you as an expert and leader, it also shines the spotlight on you and your company. Surprisingly, finding speaking opportunities isn't hard, and preparing a presentation on a topic you're familiar with shouldn't be too taxing either. It's a win-win-win if you're willing to learn to overcome the fear many people have about speaking in public.

Public presentations

The least amount of work setting up and organizing speaking opportunities lies with presentations to existing organizations comprised of your target audience. These groups have an ongoing need for speakers, which can lead to plenty of speaking gigs. Just some of the organizations you'll want to explore as possible hosts of speeches include

- **Civic organizations:** Rotary, Kiwanis, Elks, Jaycees, and other community service organizations, as well as chambers of commerce, put you in front of business leaders and potential influencers who can send business your way. Some of these groups meet weekly, thereby creating a minimum of 52 speaking opportunities each year. Take a look at your phone book directory under community service to find out which organizations have chapters in your area.

- **Professional associations:** Business groups that cater to specific types of professions and/or companies are another type of audience to explore. Skimming the *Encyclopedia of Associations* at your library gives you literally thousands of associations to target—from the National Association of Women Business Owners to the Association of Fundraising Professionals to the Professional Association of Innkeepers.

- **Trade groups:** Much like professional associations, trade groups and unions serve members of their profession, such as the Tooling and Manufacturing Association or the National Association of Women in Construction. The main difference between professional and trade organizations is that trade organizations typically serve one particular type of career, whereas professional groups are more diverse. Trade organizations also tend to consist more of blue collar workers, versus white collar.

Bright Idea

For help in improving your comfort level and public speaking skills, join Toastmasters (www.toastmasters.org). This national organization with local chapters meets regularly to give members opportunities to practice speaking before a group.

- **Educational institutions:** Schools at every level—elementary through college—routinely bring in outside speakers to address a particular topic or inspire their students in a particular area, whether it's a career choice, encouraging more volunteerism, or reporting on a particular experience you had that they might learn from. Department chairpersons are generally your best source of information regarding upcoming needs.

- **Houses of worship:** Members of churches, synagogues, and mosques, among other religious affiliations, are potential audiences for presentations.

- **Corporations:** Although to a lesser extent when the economy is struggling, corporations regularly bring in speakers to address particular divisions or groups within the organization. Training departments within companies are also charged with keeping their employees up to date and informed, which requires access to qualified speakers and instructors.

- **Seminar companies:** Companies that arrange local, regional, or national speaking engagements are another potential source of opportunities if they happen to be seeking a speaker on a topic on which you're well versed.

- **Government agencies:** Government-sponsored workshops, talks, and presentations are another venue for public speaking engagements. The key is making contact with agencies that serve your target audience or that consist of prospects.

Watch Out!

Reading from your script or notes is not okay. Members of your audience want to feel you're talking *to* them, not *at* them, and they want to see your eyes. Aim to have eye contact with members of your audience 90 to 95 percent of the time you're talking.

- **Resorts and vacation venues:** Spas, resorts, and even cruise lines have been known to bring in speakers to address their clientéle on topics of interest; some cruises even have themes, such as personal finance or a cruise for bridge players, and experts are asked to come and present to the captive audience.

- **Conventions:** Usually held at large convention halls, these meetings bring together members of a particular industry to meet, network, and learn, and they have plenty of opportunities for speakers—everything from seminar leaders to keynote speakers to breakout session facilitators. Although some conventions give preference to current industry participants, if you can demonstrate familiarity with the industry and expertise in an area of interest to its members, you may earn the chance to network with thousands of potential customers.

However, if you'd like to speak to a broader cross section of attendees or not be restricted by the requirements of an organization scheduling an event, another option is to arrange your own seminar or presentation (see the following section).

Seminars

Seminars are typically longer presentations—anywhere from an hour to an all-day session—organized to provide some knowledge or training on a particular subject. Where speeches and public presentations allow you to express an opinion or relay some useful information, a seminar is more about skill building than opinion.

Although some of the organizations listed in the preceding section do sponsor seminars, many seminars are self-organized and promoted, meaning that you need to take responsibility for developing the program, selecting the seminar location and making arrangements, promoting the seminar, and handling registrations and event set-up. Some presenters choose to offer a seminar at no cost to participants, viewing it as more of an opportunity to develop new customer relationships. Others use seminars as a profit center for the business—charging for participation and aiming to make money from the event.

There are pros and cons to both approaches, with the free seminar potentially drawing a much larger audience, and the for-profit seminar being perceived as more valuable because attendees had to pay for the information they received. The old saying, "You get what you pay for," seems to apply even to events such as seminars, where free seminars may be perceived as less valuable. Either way, seminars are an opportunity to position yourself as a knowledgeable business owner and potential resource to those in attendance and are certainly worth considering.

Courses

An even lengthier speaking opportunity is a course, such as at a school or college. If you are willing to teach others what you know about a subject and can break the information up into several individual sessions, you might consider proposing it to a local educational institution. Depending on the subject matter, the course might also work at a vocational school, recreation center, or adult education program.

Many cities have adult education outlets, such as Learning Annex, and universities with adult noncredit offerings, which are an excellent way to identify potential customers with an interest in your products or services and to demonstrate your expertise through a one-time or regular class schedule. In addition to offering your services to established adult education organizations, you can also create your own seminar or class and hold it at your place of business. Landscapers can teach about garden design, financial planners can talk about the latest savings tools for recent college grads, and personal chefs can give a cooking demonstration.

Another approach is to inquire at local schools and colleges regarding their anticipated openings for the coming year. You may learn that there are existing needs for an adjunct faculty member or visiting lecturer with your qualifications. The advantage there is that you can generally use the established curriculum as your guide, rather than having to develop an entirely new class from scratch.

Establishing an affiliation with a school or college gives you added credentials that can benefit your company, as well as potentially opening some doors through your newfound network at school. Students may become customers or clients after seeing how much you know about a particular topic.

Webinars

One of the newer variations of public speaking opportunities is the *Webinar*—a Web-based seminar. You, the speaker, can transmit audio and/or visual information, such as PowerPoint slides, through a Web site in real time to an audience of one or one thousand. Some systems have participants listen to the audio discussion via telephone, while others transmit audio to attendees through a Web site. Although attendees can't see you, they can hear you and interact with you via the telephone or e-mail.

The advantage of such seminars is that you don't need to travel and you can attract attendees from around the world, while the disadvantage is the inability of attendees to see you in person. Participants can still come away feeling very positive about you and your company, but without the live, face-to-face interaction, it's possible that impact may be lessened.

For anyone who is fearful or anxious about standing in front of a room to make a presentation, a Webinar can be a great alternative. Seated in familiar surroundings at your desk, in

Bright Idea

Check out an excellent example of a Webinar series produced by Office Depot at www.officedepot.com/renderStaticPage.do?file=/promo/webcafe/index. html&template=promo, or get to it from the main Office Depot page at www. officedepot.com. These monthly Webinars are presented by subject-matter experts and cover topics of interest to small business owners.

front of your computer instead of an audience, a Web-based seminar may be one way to build up your confidence to the point that you can attempt a live seminar. Or perhaps a Webinar can meet all your public speaking needs without increasing your anxiety level, all of which are positive outcomes.

Getting comfortable with public speaking

If you recognize the value of doing more public speaking but can't yet stomach the thought of it, there are a number of steps you can take to get past the fear and become more comfortable.

Overcoming your fear

Many people have found that it's possible to overcome a fear of public speaking. It may take a fair amount of practice, but it can be done. Here are some recommendations for reducing your anxiety about public speaking and improving your delivery:

- **Start small.** Don't overwhelm yourself with a room of hundreds of attendees. Speak first to groups of ten or twenty and work up from there.

- **Practice, practice, practice.** The more confident you are about the information you're going to give your audience, the less nervous you'll be about speaking. Know your material backward and forward, so you won't be paralyzed if you lose your place in your planned remarks. Some guidelines suggest you should put ten hours of preparation into every one hour presentation, although that may be more than you truly need. Just recognize that more practice will boost your confidence and reduce your jitters.

- **Hone your talk.** Even if you're comfortable with your speech, make sure it's a good one before potentially turning off potential customers with a bad presentation. Give it to friends and family to get feedback on how you can make it more interesting before you go public.

- **Eat something before a speech.** Although your stomach may be in knots, try to eat something small to keep your energy level up while you're presenting. If you don't, you may start to drag somewhere in the middle of your talk. Drinking wine or beer to settle your nerves is not recommended, however!

- **Arrive early for your speech or seminar.** Whether you're organizing it or have been invited by someone else to present, allow plenty of time to travel to the site and to meet and greet arrivals. Not only will you become more familiar and comfortable with the room, but you'll have the chance to chat briefly with participants. Getting to know them may help you recognize they're there to cheer you on.

- **Realize that your audience wants you to succeed.** Sometimes speakers put more pressure on themselves to be perfect than is necessary. Audiences don't expect perfection—they just want value for their time, by learning something they didn't know before. If you can provide that in an entertaining manner, you'll satisfy most of your audience. But don't worry about being perfect.

Also realize that many public personalities get nervous before speaking in public—it's part of the process of preparation. Being nervous shows that you care about doing a good job, but don't let it paralyze you.

If you're confident that you can overcome your fear, you may want to start developing a list of potential topics you're qualified to speak about.

Choosing a topic

Despite the fact that there are thousands of public speaking opportunities out there, you don't have a chance of nabbing a speaking engagement unless you follow some rules that Dottie and Lilly Walters carefully lay out in their book entitled *Speak and Grow Rich*. Although their audience is individuals interested in becoming professional speakers, the advice is useful for anyone intending to pursue speaking engagements, whether the purpose is marketing or profit:

- **Prepare material of interest to your target audience.** Don't waste your time developing presentations for groups or people who are not in your target market. Stay focused on your target customer base and the kind of information they may be interested in. Then research organizations with speaking opportunities who may consist of or cater to your target audience, but don't prepare a presentation that will be of no interest to your core audience—the one you want to sell to.

- **Listen to what the market is asking for.** What kinds of problems is your target audience facing with respect to your business? What issues are foremost in their minds? And what kinds of solutions does your company provide to your customers that you could shape into a presentation? Think about what your customers tell you they need, and then develop a presentation that discusses the challenges and solutions that are out there. Don't bother writing a speech that is of little interest to your customers—focus on the kind of information that will help them the most, and will also help position you as the go-to expert on the subject.

- **Use surveys to target topics and titles.** Dottie and Lilly Walters suggest contacting fifty people in your target market and asking them two or three questions to better understand what they're grappling with, which could be anything from hair loss to market-share loss, depending on who your audience is. By gathering information informally through a survey, you'll get a good handle on the top problems, become better known within your market simply by making contact, and have quantitative data that you can use in developing your speech. Those facts and figures your survey respondents share with you can be woven throughout your presentation to demonstrate how well you know your market and how well you've come up with solutions to their problems.

- **Check the bestseller lists.** The lists of bestselling books published weekly by newspapers like *The New York Times* are an indicator of what topics are hot right now, with both consumers and businesses. Just look to the nonfiction or self-help categories to learn what issues people are struggling with. And the business nonfiction category is a snapshot of what executives may be pondering. Use that information to brainstorm potential presentation topics that link these current hot buttons with your company's products and services.

- **Profit from the flip side of topics.** Sometimes, examining the polar opposite of a topic or issue can be a goldmine. Turning a topic around and approaching it from an innovative perspective can often catch the attention of potential attendees and help establish you as the expert on the topic, because everyone else is tackling it from the same vantage point. For example, instead of speaking about the importance of customer retention to business success—which sounds rather obvious—how about developing a talk on how firing customers can make businesses even more successful?

- **Always look for new topic ideas.** Topic ideas won't always come to you; you may have to go looking, such as by chatting with attendees and speakers at other conferences and meetings, eavesdropping on conversations about your customers' pet peeves, and taking note of what's happening in other industries.

After you've chosen a topic for your speech, come up with a clever title that really grabs your audience's attention, such as a play on words, use of a cliché, reference to pop culture or current events, or industry jargon. A title can really get people talking about your speech even before you've stepped up to the podium, giving you extra marketing value. For example, if you're talking about new discoveries in astronomy, you might call it "To Infinity and Beyond," a la Buzz Lightyear in *Toy Story,* while a talk about sugar addiction might be called "Finding your Way out of Candyland."

Preparing a presentation

As you get ready for your presentation, keep in mind your attire. You want to convey that you are successful and professional, so be sure your clothing is in sync with that image. Of course, what is appropriate will vary according to the place and audience you're speaking to—a suit and tie is best for a business luncheon but shorts and a shirt are more appropriate for a boat tour. Women should also take care not to appear too trendy, sexy, or frumpy—clothing should have full coverage.

To get the most value from the time and energy you'll spend identifying, pursuing, and giving speeches, take some time to make the best possible impression on your audience, which you hope includes customers, prospects, and people who can influence others to consider buying from you. Do a bang-up job giving a speech, and you may get fans swarming you at its completion, eager to buy what you're selling—whether it's advice on dating or the latest home-protection device. So that you give the best speech you can, take a look through the following tips.

Start strong

The first minute or two of your presentation is your chance to hook your audience and reel them in with a personal story or anecdote.

In addition to setting the tone for your talk—will it be humorous, inspirational, chock-full of useful tidbits?—a story will engage your listeners and help them connect with you, especially if the story is true. With an interesting tale, you can make a point, teach a lesson, and help attendees feel that they've gotten to know you.

Whatever you do, refrain from using well-known jokes to lead off your presentation. You'll lose the respect of your audience for repeating a tired or offensive gem (remember that what you may think is funny and what they may think is funny may not mesh). In addition, you'll position yourself as a comedian, not as an expert with useful information to share with them.

Introduce your main points

You've probably heard the advice that when making a speech or presentation, you should tell the audience what you're going to tell them, tell them, and then remind them of what you've just told them. It's good advice. So before you launch into your tips, observations, or arguments, briefly give an overview so that your audience knows what's coming next.

Elaborate

Use a story for each lesson or point you want to make. Stories help listeners remember the material much more clearly. Weave

---

 Money Saver

Before you spend your time and money copying handouts or printing overhead cells for your presentation, ask your host (that is, your contact at the organization that has invited you to speak) whether he or she can make copies and handle any production issues for you. Most will say yes.

Bright Idea

Before you start greeting arriving guests and attendees, take a minute to confirm that the sound system is working properly and that you know how to turn it on and operate it.

in facts and figures to support your story and to drive home the conclusion you want participants to reach at the end of each anecdote.

Keep the tone conversational

Most people don't want to be lectured to or talked at—they want to get involved in the discussion, or at least feel a connection with the speaker. Talk to them as if they are all long-time friends who know you well; leave out the jargon or formal language that can get in the way of comprehension and make you sound haughty or egotistical—neither of which you want.

Include the audience

If you arrive early and have the chance to mix and mingle with attendees as they file in, try to catch some names and background information from some of the folks. Then, as you're talking, sprinkle in examples from your audience, even if it's a quick mention. You'll impress everyone, and they'll feel even more a part of the presentation.

You can also ask questions before, during, or after the talk, to find out about your audience members. Learning more about their biggest challenges, the types of jobs they have, or what kinds of companies they work for, for example, may be useful information you can use to tailor your presentation to their backgrounds and experience. Or you can use questions to provide concrete examples of points you're trying to make—get your participants to help you make those points, and you'll leave an even stronger impression.

Bright Idea

If you find you're scheduled to make several presentations or speeches, set aside space on your Web site to trumpet those events. Create a list of upcoming talks for fans who might like to hear your presentation, and to reinforce that expert image—you're in demand!

Use visual aids selectively

Projection devices, overhead machines, and flipcharts can be a big help when making a complex presentation, but don't rely on them too much. Visual aids are most effective at illustrating a particular point here and there, but be aware that they can also shift your attendees' attention away from you. Try to keep your attendees engrossed in the stories you have to tell, not the Excel file you created and have displayed on the wall.

On the other hand, people love to see things up close, or to hold them in their hands, so bring along samples of your products, photocopies of a relevant magazine article, or templates for attendees to follow later. These *take-aways* allow attendees to carry their enthusiasm for your program home or back to the office. Some speakers prefer to wait until the end of a program to hand out such items for fear that their audience will become so fascinated with the freebie that they'll stop listening to what is being said. And the rustling of papers can be very distracting!

Don't rely too heavily on note cards or papers

If you hyperventilate at the mere suggestion of giving a speech, you may want to bring along crutches to calm your nerves—crutches like note cards and a script. Reviewing your notes before you begin speaking is fine, but if you lay it in front of you, you may find yourself reading your notes instead of using them for reference, and reading is the kiss of death as far as your audience is concerned. Reading your notes also reduces the positive marketing value of speaking in public, because it suggests to those in attendance that you don't know your subject well enough to talk off the cuff. You appear to be less of an expert if all you're going to do is read, rather than speak from memory.

And that's the key to making the most of public speaking opportunities—coming across as an expert to those who are there to hear you. Being perceived as an expert will make them more likely to hire you to tackle their problems, whatever they are, and they will be more likely to recommend you to others facing similar challenges. And unlike one-on-one meetings with prospects, public speaking enables you to speak to hundreds or thousands of people at one time, making it one of the most efficient marketing methods around.

Invite questions

Allow time at the end of your speech for questions from the audience. This ensures they will walk away with their concerns addressed, which heightens their satisfaction with your talk, and makes for some lively conversation.

Just the facts

- Speaking in public is an excellent way to position yourself as an expert in your field, and, by extension, your company as a leader. And because people prefer to deal with people they respect, you enhance your brand image every time you speak in public—assuming you do a good job.

- Some people fear public speaking more than death. If you fall into this category, you have two choices: Work to get over your fear so that you can tap into this marketing technique, or flip to Chapter 12 and don't waste time pursuing such opportunities.

- One of the best ways to beat, or at least reduce, a fear of public speaking is to invest considerable time in preparing for a presentation. The more confident you are that you know your material, the more relaxed you can be about your performance. But don't put too much pressure on yourself to be perfect—no one expects it.

- The best topics are those that relate to your company in some way and can help convince customers to do business with you. Taking a controversial perspective or a counter-intuitive approach to a topic can also be of interest to participants. But make sure they all reflect positively on your company—avoid bashing or trash talking competitors.

- The best speakers connect with the members of their audience; appear to be talking off the top of their head, rather than having their head buried in their notes; and use stories and anecdotes to illustrate three to five major points—no more.

Moderately Priced Marketing Approaches

GET THE SCOOP ON...
Spreading your marketing message electronically ■
Knowing why a Web site is essential ■
Connecting with customers online ■ Discovering
e-zines, Weblogs, and podcasts

PART IV

Online Marketing

Chapter 10

The Internet has completely changed how business is done—from how companies market their products and services to how information is gathered by consumers to where sales are transacted. It's also a powerful equalizer. Today, even the smallest of businesses can tap into the potential sales the World Wide Web offers by attracting, informing, and selling to anyone in the world with Internet access. The potential for growth is tremendous.

Marketing via the Internet can be cost efficient, effective, fast, and profitable when done properly. But it can also be costly and a waste of time. Not all online tools are appropriate for your company, but some can significantly boost the number of leads you receive and the number of qualified prospects you hear from and can help reduce your sales cycle. It's a powerful marketing tool you definitely want to explore.

The best online tool:
Your Web site

The one online tool you don't want to ignore is a Web site. Although years ago the only businesses with Web sites were retailers that wanted to sell beyond their immediate area, a Web site today is a smart investment for companies of all sizes, in all industries, because it can do the following:

- Help customers find you
- Inform potential customers about your products and services
- Allow customers to research your products on their own
- Alert customers to your hours and payment options
- Demonstrate your experience
- Convey the benefits of working with you
- Showcase successful work you've done for other people or companies
- Prove that you're serious about your business
- Build credibility for your company
- Qualify potential customers
- Educate customers about the many options they have available
- Explain why your company is the best to buy from
- Position you and your business as a leader in your industry
- Provide a platform from which you can distribute information electronically
- Align your company with other businesses through online links
- Allow customers to buy from you

Certainly, your Web site can also serve as an online retail storefront if you're planning to sell products directly from your Web site. But that's only one of many possible reasons to invest in designing, programming, and hosting a Web site.

Money Saver

One of the first things you'll want to do as you plan your Web site is to reserve a domain name. To make it easy for customers to find you, stick with a name that mirrors your company's name, or at least is darn close. GoDaddy (www.godaddy.com) is one of the cheapest places to register your name, with rates as low as $6.95 a year.

A Web site is the hub of your online marketing program. Not only is it the place where prospects can learn more about you, but it can also capture information from potential customers through a registration process.

Be aware that most people hate to have to provide personal information in order to register, so the fewer the questions you ask, the better your chances of identifying who has been to your site. For example, simply asking visitors to provide their e-mail address will be much less onerous to them than asking for their mailing address and phone number. Keep it simple, and you'll gather more names and e-mail addresses.

Many companies have found that Web sites can significantly reduce the number of routine phone calls they receive regarding store hours and location, as well as offering possible solutions to customer service issues and technical problems, all without human involvement. Think, for example, of the amount of technical information you can read and download from major computer manufacturer Web sites, thereby reducing your potential need for live assistance, which costs them more to provide.

Starting with a simple Web site structure

Although major corporations create Web sites with hundreds or thousands of different online pages, your Web site can be extremely simple and still be effective. Basic pages you'll want to include are as follows:

- **Home page:** This first page is where potential customers land when they arrive at your site. You'll want to have a brief statement somewhere on this page summarizing what you do, perhaps using images or photos related to your company. The home page is also where you identify the other sections of your Web site that guests may want to check into.

- **About Us:** This page is a brief write-up providing some history of your company, information on the products and services offered, who started the company and who is leading it now, and what makes your business different from the rest. This is also the place to quote your customers: What do your customers rave about, and why do new customers choose to do business with your company versus others?

- **Product or service description:** In some cases, one page is all you need to summarize what you offer, and in other cases, you may need several, especially if you have several lines of business, such as products, consulting services, subscription offerings, and so on. Each of those lines should have its own Web page on your site.

- **Contact:** Sometimes all anyone needs is a phone number, a street address, or an e-mail address, and this section, which need only be one short page, can provide contact information. If you can make it easier, by providing a hot link that generates a pop-up e-mail screen, so much the better. Some companies build in a response form for people to fill out, which generates a message that gets sent to the appropriate person from that page, but they are less helpful in small-business settings.

  Consumers today expect near-instantaneous responses to e-mail messages. To allay any fears that you didn't receive their message, set up an *automatic responder* (auto-responder for short) that automatically replies to confirm that you received the e-mail and will get back within a certain number of hours. Then respond even more quickly than promised, to exceed their expectations.

Bright Idea

Before you spend time and money setting up photo shoots to capture rather generic images, such as a crowd of people, for example, take a look at stock photographs that have already been taken and are available for a fee. You can often save time and money by paying for the usage of an image, or images, rather than paying for a totally new image to be taken. Getty Images, at www.gettyimages.com, is one of the largest suppliers.

Beyond the basics: Additional Web design options

Some companies find that a bare-bones Web site isn't enough, either because there is much more information their customers want to access online, or because more information suggests a thriving and successful business, and they want to present that image.

Other pages to include

Other pages (sections) you may want to consider creating include

- **Audio or video files:** Although audio or video files take up a considerable amount of computing space, allowing your Web site visitors to click and watch your most recent appearance on *The Today Show* or hear your latest radio interview may be worth the extra cost.

- **Clients:** A list of customers or clients you've worked with builds credibility with potential customers, especially in business-to-business selling. You'll want to check first that it's okay to include each company's name, however. For privacy reasons, listing individuals' names isn't recommended.

- **Links to other sites:** If you've identified organizations that have information or resources of potential value to your customers and other Web visitors, offering a link to that information, or a live feed to your site, could help establish your business as being well connected and familiar with the interests of your customer base.

Watch Out!

Although listing big-name clients will win you credibility, be careful about getting too specific when citing company names. Your competition may add your clients to their prospect list, so don't make it too easy for them to go after that business by mentioning the specific contact person.

- **News:** If you distribute press releases and announcements regularly, having a section of your Web site for people to access this information can be helpful, especially to members of the press. Here, you can also highlight recent articles in which you've been quoted, if that's a part of your business.

- **Success stories:** Customers may feel more confident about working with you or buying from you if they know you've had success tackling similar situations—whether it's a great haircut, designing a custom wedding ring, or interfacing one enterprise computing system with another—for other customers. This section can provide brief summaries of the results you've achieved for other clients, using words or photos.

- **Technical support:** If you sell a product, having helpful tips for difficulties your customers frequently encounter can reduce their frustration level and reduce the number of phone calls your company receives. Some companies use an FAQ (frequently asked questions) section to deal with the most common problems or complaints.

- **Testimonials:** When your customers would prefer that you not detail exactly what you've done for them, perhaps because you're a turnaround specialist, bankruptcy attorney, or plastic surgeon, short testimonials can often work just as well. Without getting into specifics, customers can rave about what you do best and why they're delighted they chose you in the first place.

Bright Idea

After your Web site is up and running, set up an e-mail address at your new site's URL, such as me@mywebsite.com. It's much more professional than an e-mail address at Hotmail or Yahoo!

- **Work samples:** A section that shows samples of your work is especially useful for artisans and firms that develop custom products, to help customers decide whether your style matches what they're looking for.

Creating a Web site from scratch can take anywhere from a couple of weeks to several months, depending on how large the site is, how sophisticated or technical some of the online tools are (such as a registration page or pdf documents available for download), and how easy the images are to choose and pull together. The three basic participants in the creation of any Web site are the designer, who determines your site's look; the writer, who crafts the brilliant statements about your business; and the photographer—often working closely with the designer, who chooses and arranges to obtain the necessary photos and images. Sometimes, the Web designer can also serve as photographer, or can find existing images, reducing the number of parties involved to two.

Then again, many small business owners create basic Web sites themselves at little or no cost. Guides such as the one at www.webdesign.about.com can be useful in selecting the best online tools for your needs.

 Money Saver

After you've developed your site, you'll want to be sure the major search engines are able to find it. Although you can pay $50 to $200 to a firm to handle all the listings yourself, you can also head to the Help section of each search engine individually, such as Google and Yahoo!, and enter the information for free. Sure, it's time-consuming, but it doesn't cost you anything.

Bringing visitors back for more

As you're planning your site, one challenge to work on is how you'll encourage visitors to come back. The most effective Web sites are those that draw people back regularly—the more frequently the better. The reason is that the more interactions someone has with your site, the more familiar they are with, and the more positive their perception of, your company.

Some strategies for bringing folks back again and again, which you'll want to build in up front, include the following:

- **Contests:** A simple, random drawing of everyone who registers at the site in a given month is one approach, perhaps offering a gift card as the prize. Or you can get more complicated and require some action on your visitors' part, such as answering a series of questions about your company or finding a particular icon or clue hidden at the site.

- **Discussion forums:** Creating a special chat area where customers and other visitors can come and hang out with each other electronically, or communicate via listserv, is another way to hook them. Becoming part of an online community is a big benefit if the discussions are useful and interesting.

- **Games:** Interactive gaming is big right now and will only get bigger. Creating your own game for visitors to play will bring them back, but it could cost you some serious cash to develop. Simpler, fill-in-the-blank formats, such as a build-your-own press release for an advertising agency or a quick quiz, should be much easier to develop.

- **Hard-to-find information:** Ultimately, this is what makes your site distinctive and unique and will bring visitors back. If you can become a repository of information about job openings in your field, for example, or upcoming special events, that's yet another reason for guests to check back with you.

Bright Idea

Keep tabs on what keyword searches bring visitors to your site, as well as where they come from and where they go, by reviewing your Web site statistics each month. Your hosting company keeps track of all that information—just make sure your contract provides for that level of detailed information.

- **Live chat:** If you schedule one time a month, for example, when you'll be online to answer customer questions personally, you may entice customers to participate who have questions to ask of you.

- **New information:** If your company positions itself as *the* place to turn for the latest information in your field, you need to back that up with regular facts, reports, and tidbits your customers want to know.

- **Special offers:** Monthly coupons or biweekly promotions available online, or with a coupon generated at your site, are all reasons for shoppers to return regularly.

- **Surveys:** People love to express their opinions, which is what online polls and surveys allow. Some companies take quick polls of their visitors, and then publicly report the results each week, or month, while others develop a survey purely for the personal enjoyment of their guests, such as calculating your emotional intelligence, for example.

Exploring your hosting options

As you're working to get your Web site ready for its public debut, you also want to evaluate your many Web hosting options. Hosting companies provide the computing space where your Web site actually resides, and you pay a monthly fee for that service. Depending on how much space you need, based on how large your site is, whether you need 24-hour customer support by phone, and how many e-mail addresses you want to associate with your Web site, the fees will vary widely. Your best bet is to ask your Web designer for recommendations or call local Web design firms and ask their opinions.

Driving traffic to your site

After you've built your Web site, your next task is to find ways to get new people to visit. Just creating your Web site and making it available for viewing isn't enough to generate business from it. You need to let everyone know that it's there.

One way to point customers your way is to pay for online advertising at some of the major search engines—mainly Google and Yahoo!. With online ads at these sites, you specify keywords that trigger your ad to appear on the page, and you pay for each visitor who clicks through to check out your Web site. You can set a budget that controls how much you spend per month, and you can cancel whenever you want, which is a big plus. And with per-click fees that can start at just a few cents, it's fairly easy to keep your expenses low. And some companies are finding the payoff is big. Very big.

For a mere $5 a day, HarpWorld, Inc. of Anaheim, California, has watched its Web site traffic jump by hundreds more hits a month. The company, which is partnered with Salvi Harps of Italy, decided in 2005 to invest in a Google AdWords campaign. As a result, HarpWorld has seen a significant increase in site visits and has landed at least one sale as a direct result. Although linking sales to any one particular marketing method is nearly impossible, the company knows that at least one harp sale occurred as a result of the client spotting the Google ad. And given that harps can sell for anywhere from $3,000 to $90,000, it's safe to say that the company's AdWords cost has been more than covered for years to come, all from that one sale.

HarpWorld initially started with one ad group, which appears along the side of or across the page of a Google search results page, but saw few results. But after consulting with the Google AdWords team, they upgraded to a set of three ads—all the same—that run together. In fact, they have 18 different variations of these ads, which are now performing better than anticipated, and HarpWorld is considering increasing its AdWords budget because of the positive response.

Digitally communicating your message

For online marketers, a Web site is like home base. All marketing either begins or ends at the site, which is why it is so important.

But in order to get the most value out of the investment in your Web site, you'll want to strike up an ongoing conversation with people who have visited your site, or who have indicated an interest in your company. After someone becomes a prospect or customer, you'll want to solidify that new relationship you've started by staying in touch and by encouraging that prospect to make other purchases in the future.

Some of the ways companies are staying in touch these days include electronic newsletters, called e-zines (pronounced EE-zeens); blogs, short for Weblogs; and podcasts, which are transmitted to MP3 users. There are format challenges with each, but the biggest cost to use these tools is time—that is, your time coming up with worthwhile information to share.

E-zines

In the 1990s, the hottest marketing tool around was the newsletter. Businesses of all shapes and sizes were suddenly creating and mailing newsletters to their prospects and customers. They became extremely popular because they worked—done well, newsletters brought customers back for more.

 Watch Out!

Before lifting information you've spotted elsewhere, such as a cartoon or an article, be sure you request and receive permission from the owner to reuse that material. Simply copying other articles is copyright infringement and can open you up to expensive lawsuits for stealing.

Bright Idea

Another digital marketing tool to consider is the compact disc (CD), which is a cost-effective and easy way to provide background information about your business as well as work samples tailored to your prospect's specific interests, needs, or situation. Such flexibility is in contrast to more traditional print brochures and materials, which cannot be updated or changed after they're produced.

Customers enjoyed receiving them from companies they knew because they provided new product information and promotions, offered helpful tips, and included useful information not found anywhere else. Some were four-color glossy versions stapled together, while others were of the simple two-page variety with black text and folded in half. The format and appearance mattered much less than the information the newsletter contained.

In time, however, newsletters became so common and plentiful that recipients had to start weeding through the ones they would spend time on and those they wouldn't. Response rates fell as competition for readers' time rose, and some companies stopped sending newsletters altogether.

Today, newsletters are back in vogue in a new format—electronic—with a new name, the e-zine. Why spend money printing and mailing a newsletter when you can simply hit "send" on your computer and have your electronic newsletter sitting in inboxes worldwide, at no additional cost. Sure, you still have to write and lay out the information, but production costs have plummeted to the point that any size small business can afford to send one.

Knowing what to include

"But what would I say?" you may be wondering. It's true, coming up with interesting information on a regular basis is a challenge, and when you commit to a newsletter—whether it's weekly, monthly, bimonthly, or occasionally—you need to live up to the commitment you've made to your prospects and customers.

To get you started, here are some types of articles or tidbits you can include in your own e-zine:

- **A personal note** from you, the owner, with news of recent accomplishments or exciting new products or a new report confirming the usefulness of your services

- **News pieces** that announce new products, new services, a special event, an important piece of legislation, or a milestone, for example; keep the tone as newsy as possible, rather than self-promotional and sales-y

- **Profiles** of satisfied customers who have achieved great results through the use of your products or services and who are willing to talk about the difference your company made in their lives or their business; similar to testimonials, but they include specifics about what customers bought and how they used those products or services

- **How-to information** that helps readers make better use of your product or service, or that helps them with a related challenge; for example, if you sell hot tubs, you could include articles on keeping hot tubs clean, avoiding costly maintenance, finding the best spots to locate hot tubs in and around your home, as well as topics related to stress reduction, healthy living, and relaxation

- **Research or survey results** related to your business or to issues your customers routinely face; in business-to-business newsletters, for example, articles on time management and organization are always a hit because no one has enough time to get everything done

- **Answer frequently asked questions** (FAQs) in a question-and-answer (Q&A) format, with the question posed, followed by your response

Money Saver

Where banner ads were a form of currency in the early days of the Internet, and companies agreed to feature ads on their Web site in exchange for a similar treatment on other Web sites, today companies trade e-mail distribution lists with a note endorsing their partner company. What companies have complementary products or services that you could partner with and swap e-mail promotions?

Although print newsletters have traditionally been a very soft sell, including little or no promotional information, e-zines today are much more promotional, often containing special offers for readers. Some also contain ads either inserted in boxes throughout the text or at the end of the e-zine. But be careful not to be too promotional, or the information will be quickly discarded.

Appearance is also less important with e-zines than with print newsletters, and many are sent out purely as text documents (with little or no formatting, images, or design) to be sure that all recipients will be able to read it. Keep in mind that readers not set up to read HTML code are unable to decipher newsletters that contain images or special formatting.

Building your e-zine distribution list

To build your e-zine distribution list, offer a free subscription to your newsletter on the home page of your Web site and suggest that anyone interested in receiving it sign up there. Not only will you give people a reason to check out your Web site, but your Web site can serve as the central point of contact for your business—as it should be.

In addition to providing a place for Web visitors to opt-in to request your e-zine, you also need to provide a way for them to unsubscribe to (or opt-out of) future mailings. You also need a clearly communicated privacy policy, so that visitors know how their personal information—generally their e-mail addresses—will be used.

Blogs

Where an e-zine generally has a schedule for distribution, a Weblog (blog for short) does not. *Blogs* are ongoing editorial commentary that are supplemented (that is, added to) whenever the writer feels so inclined. They are personal journal entries, really, that are typed up and featured at a particular Internet address, which can be linked to your corporate Web site.

A blog, which is similar to an electronic newspaper column, is very easy to set up and provides a forum where the writer can share insights, musings, and commentary to give customers a better sense of the personality of the blogger—who can be you or someone else on your team—and his or her opinions on topics related to the company and its industry.

A blog can appear on a Web site, providing regular updates or tips for customers, for example, or separately, at a different address provided by the blogging Web site used. You can set up a blog for free at www.blogger.com/start.

Some bloggers post daily, keeping their readers well informed of what's on their minds, while other bloggers write when something occurs that they believe is relevant to their audience. Because visitors are in control of when they check out a blog, frequency is less of an issue than with e-zines, which are distributed. Readers can visit a blog and read all the past postings at one time, or only the most recent one. However, the more frequent your entries, the more likely you'll draw people back to the site to read your material.

Although blogs are much more casual than other forms of writing, you'll want to keep in mind the following tips, from Sandra Beckwith, author of *Streetwise Complete Publicity Plans: How to Create Publicity That Will Spark Media Exposure and Excitement:*

- Remember that your blog postings are an extension of your reputation and of your company's image. Be careful that what you say doesn't burn any bridges.

- Watch for spelling, grammar, and punctuation errors that would damage your credibility.

- You wouldn't write and send an e-mail when you're angry, so don't write in your blog when you're angry.

- Post regularly—anything less than once or twice a week probably isn't enough.

- You can decide whether to allow people to add comments to your postings. You can also decide whether you want to respond to those comments (some you probably shouldn't).

To learn more about the types of blogs that are currently being written, and by whom, visit www.blogwise.com, which is a directory of blogs worldwide.

Podcasts

Whereas blogs allow you to communicate using on-screen text, *podcasts* use audio files that your audience listens to using an Apple iPod or other MP3 player. The audio files are made available on your Web site and can then be played on customers' desktop computers or downloaded to an MP3 player.

In addition to music, the most popular form of audio file, you can also download podcasts about everything from politics to cooking to sports to entertainment. Nearly all are free—another big plus. And although a radio program format is quite popular, you don't have to stick to that. You can give a weekly tip or suggestion, or set up a question-and-answer session with an expert. How you decide to present the information on your topic is up to you, and you may even want to try out a few different strategies before settling on one.

The one thing you'll want to do before you start recording is to settle on a theme for your podcasts. What will all your recordings have in common? What will you promise your audience in terms of information or style or entertainment? How will you maintain a link between your business and your podcast—after all, marketing your business is your main objective here.

To get started in podcasting doesn't require a lot of expensive equipment, but there are a few must-haves:

- A computer running on a newer version of Windows, Mac OS X, or Linux

- An Internet connection

- A microphone that plugs into your computer and costs around $30

- Sound recording software, which can be downloaded for free at http://audacity.sourceforge.net and works on both PCs and Macs

- An MP3 encoder, which converts your file into an MP3 format; a free one, the LAME MP3 Encoder, can be downloaded at www.free-codecs.com/Lame_Encoder_download.htm

A fairly easy-to-follow guide for recording and converting your audio file to MP3 format is available on Yahoo! at http://podcasts.yahoo.com/publish.

If the iPod's popularity is any indication of how and where consumers will be listening to information, podcasts will certainly be the wave of the future.

Even if your business is not high tech, making use of high-tech marketing tools, such as a Web site, blog, or podcast, makes a positive impression on potential customers who are assessing your capabilities. And as increasing numbers of business people and consumers make purchasing decisions online, or based on information they find online, investing in online marketing becomes even more essential.

 Bright Idea

When your podcast is available for download, announce it to the world by listing it in one of several podcast directories. You can find a list at help.yahoo.com/l/us/yahoo/podcasts/podcasts-52692.html.

Just the facts

- At the core of your online marketing efforts is a Web site to which you can direct prospects, customers, and the media. The Web site should have a minimum of four pages: a home page; an About Us page that gives a brief company bio; a page where you describe your products or services; and a Contact page where you indicate how customers can get in touch with you.

- Your Web site should allow those who visit it to quickly understand what your company does, know why they would want to work with you, and leave with a positive impression of your business.

- All your marketing should direct prospects and customers to visit your Web site for more information, but to proactively communicate with that audience, use an electronic newsletter, or e-zine. E-zines are inexpensive to set up and provide an opportunity for companies to routinely inform their target audiences about events and topics of interest.

- A blog, short for Weblog, is a personal journal you update frequently with thoughts and observations that your target audience is interested in. Setting up a blog is free and easy and provides another reason for your prospects and customers to come back to your Web site.

- With more consumers becoming attached to mobile MP3 players, which play audio files, the demand for audio content is increasing rapidly. Regular broadcasts of audio material for use by iPod and MP3 users are called podcasts, and are another way for you to keep in touch with your audience. You can make free podcasts available for download at your Web site using a tutorial at http://podcasts.yahoo.com/publish.

Chapter 11

GET THE SCOOP ON...
Producing basic printed pieces you shouldn't be
without ▪ Developing materials for every occasion ▪ Understanding important factors before
going to print ▪ Finding tips for saving money

Printed Pieces

E ven in the digital age, printed business literature is still important—even expected. The
design, photos, paper quality, size, and printing
are clues to your company's success, professionalism,
market stature, and taste, among other things. Your
printed pieces are a reflection of your company, so
choose wisely.

Of course, some printed materials are more
important than others, with letterhead, envelopes,
and business cards at the top of the list, and promotional pieces like trade show bags and posters at the
bottom. Sure, they're nice to have and support your
company's identity, but they won't make or break
your business like the lack of a business card will.

Must have: The basics

Despite our entry into the electronic age, some
paper-based marketing tools remain the gold standard: business cards, stationery, mailing envelopes,
and labels. In some cases, brochures, too. Yes, it's
possible to design digital, Internet-based versions of
each of these, but so far, the traditional hard copy

form of the pieces listed is still preferred by the majority of Americans. Be sure you invest in well-designed and -produced variations of these marketing materials.

Business cards

If you choose to invest in only one type of printed marketing materials, let it be a business card. Your business card is likely your most-used tool. You should be handing them out whenever you meet someone new and whenever you mail out correspondence. Most small business owners go through hundreds of cards per year, although, granted, there are some types of businesses for which a business card may be less important, such as a restaurant, where menus would be at the top of their list of essentials. But even a restaurant can benefit from a business card that features its phone number for take-out or lists its daily specials on the back.

Designing your card

Your business card represents your company's image. For this reason, even if you're just starting out, hire a graphic designer to create a business card that presents a positive image of you and your business. Yes, a graphic designer costs money, but in many cases, he or she can also save you money by helping you get the best deal at the printer. A well-designed business card protects your image and helps you attract customers, rather than turning them off with an amateurish card that shows you cut corners. Is that the first impression you want to give customers—that you settle for the cheapest alternative? Few companies benefit by presenting a business card that looks homemade or is printed on perforated sheets on an inkjet printer. It doesn't inspire confidence that the company will be in business long-term.

Knowing what information to include

No matter what approach you take to presenting the information on your business card, the essential pieces of information to include are as follows:

- Your name
- Your title
- Your company's name
- Your company's logo, if you have one
- Your street or mailing address
- Your phone number
- Your fax number
- Your cell phone number, if you give it out
- Your e-mail address
- Your company's Web site address

However, it's often the additional information that makes your card, and potentially your business, a stand-out. Examples of other useful pieces of information to consider including somewhere on the card—front or back—include the following:

- A small map to your location
- Hours of operation
- Credit cards accepted
- Services offered
- Honors and awards—special award logos are especially effective
- Association memberships
- A slogan or *tag line,* which is a short sentence or phrase that summarizes your business's mission or services
- Special offers or discounts

 Money Saver

If you're interested in having a professional graphic designer create your business card, approach a local college's graphic arts department to see whether any of the professors are willing to take on your design as a class project. It will take a little longer, but the design will be free. You could also ask for a recommendation of a top design student and offer to pay him or her to prepare yours for far less than you'd pay for a practicing professional.

Although the standard business card is 3" x 2", some businesses opt for a smaller or larger card as a means of standing out, or go for a fold-over that gives more space for information. This is certainly an option for you as well, but be aware that some people still file their cards in devices, such as Rolodex files or plastic file cases, with standard business-card-size openings. Cards that don't fit are either tossed or filed away somewhere else—not exactly the best way to stay at the top of your customers' minds.

Choosing card stock and colors

Before you go to print, you'll need to choose a paper stock and colors. Of course, the thicker the paper you choose and the more ink colors involved, the higher the printing cost.

Choose a paper weight—card stock, preferably—that feels good in your hand. You may also want to think ahead to your letterhead, if you haven't already, and choose a paper variety that will look nice with your stationery.

Four-color printing used to be more expensive than using one or two colors, but today, the difference is much smaller. However, a good graphic designer can also make a one or two-color card look luxurious and impressive. And unless you plan on featuring your photo or a product image, you probably don't really need four colors of ink anyway.

Deciding how many to print

Before starting up the printing presses, calculate how many cards you expect to go through in a year and print up a few extras. It costs far more to re-set up the printer and print more

 Watch Out!

Choosing a predesigned card stock from a catalog, or having free business cards printed off the Internet, is also risky, because your card will now look like many other cards out there. Yours won't be the least bit distinctive and will show that you focused on saving money instead of making a good impression. Printing up a bunch of brochures or cards every time you need them is also not the best use of your time.

cards later than it does to run a few more now. A box of 500 or 1,000 cards wouldn't be out of line.

Stationery

One of the most important words in marketing is consistency. Carrying the look and feel of your business card over to your company's letterhead and envelope reinforces the image you're striving for. If your business card and your stationery (both your letterhead and envelope) look like they came from different companies and/or have radically different designs, you have a problem. Every piece of information your customers receive from you should have the same look and feel to reinforce your company name and image and help build familiarity and a comfort level with you. (See Chapter 15 for more on branding.) Over time, that comfort level turns to trust, which increases the chances of a sale.

An inconsistent set of marketing materials damages your credibility and ends up costing you money, because it will take more direct contacts before customers become familiar with your business. In the advertising world, it is believed that a customer must see an ad seven or eight times before he or she will consider buying from you—it takes that many occurrences to build familiarity, then recognition, and then trust and consideration. So the more you can do to make your marketing materials look consistent, the quicker your potential customers will hit the magic number: seven or eight.

But consistency doesn't have to mean matchy-matchy. The paper you use for your business card doesn't have to match exactly your letterhead and envelope, but it should certainly complement it, either through the color, texture, or design. The set should look like it goes together.

When designing your letterhead, or having a graphic designer create it, include the same basic information as is on your business card. Make sure that if someone were to receive a letter on your stationery, he or she would be able to respond to you via phone, fax, or e-mail easily, using contact information you supply on the page.

Bright Idea

One of the most eye-catching elements of any of your marketing materials is your logo. Don't have one? Pay a designer to create one, unless you are a professional designer yourself. A logo communicates the style and character of your business in an instant and will become the most recognized part of all your marketing efforts. But have your logo created first—before you invest in printing any of your marketing materials. One company that specializes in logos is LogoWorks at www.logoworks.com.

Mailing labels

Although not officially part of a stationery *package,* which consists of business cards, letterhead, and envelopes, having mailing labels printed that coordinate with the rest of your materials is a nice touch. You may find a number of uses for them beyond adorning a mailing envelope, such as turning pocket folders into information packets or media kits, labeling CD cases, placing them on the front of three-ring binders, as well as adhering them to boxes and packages.

Helpful to have

Although some marketing pieces are critical, others are nice to have, but not necessary. The following pieces can boost the effectiveness of your marketing program, but in many cases, you can wait until money becomes available or a specific need arises to produce them.

Note cards

Personal notes strike a chord with people, whether you're talking about a customer or your grandmother. People like to get handwritten notes; it makes them feel more positively about the person who sent it. For this reason, send out personal notes at every opportunity. Possible occasions include the following:

- A customer's birthday
- A promotion
- A recent sizeable purchase from you
- A new home
- A wedding
- A new baby
- A child's or grandchild's graduation
- An illness
- The mention of a customer in the newspaper
- An award or honor
- The holidays

The holidays are one of the most popular occasions for sending cards to customers. Some companies budget hundreds of dollars to have cards custom designed with seasons' greetings.

Although I don't recommend this expenditure for a small business with limited funds, I suggest that note cards with your company's logo embossed or imprinted on the front cover is a good use of funds. Such versatile cards will be quickly used for more purposes than I've listed in this section and will serve to remind the recipient of how thoughtful you are.

The cost to print one-color note cards with matching envelopes should not be more than a couple hundred dollars—probably less.

 Bright Idea

Because most companies send out holiday greetings at the end of the year, your business will stand out if you send out notes at other times, such as Thanksgiving, the Fourth of July, or even the first day of school, to express your appreciation for their business.

Newsletters

Newsletters have broad appeal and can be used by nearly any type of organization. Doctors; dentists; financial planners; personal trainers; companies that manufacture toys, diapers, and cars; drapery makers; cabinet designers; and marketing consultants all use newsletters to encourage their customers and prospects to do business with them. And in many cases, it works. See Chapter 10 for the lowdown on electronic newsletters, called e-zines.

A newsletter's primary purpose is to maintain contact with customers and keep the company's name top-of-mind, but it can also generate interest in new products and services, educate customers, and announce important events or specials. Information often featured in a newsletter includes the following:

- Changes to company policies
- Company announcements and good news
- Honors, awards, and certifications earned
- How-to information to help customers make better use of the company's products or services
- Industry facts and figures
- Instructions for maintaining or trouble-shooting a particular product
- Message from the president or owner
- Information about new employees or promotions
- New products or services being introduced
- Recommended resources
- Reports or research results
- Short survey or poll you conduct
- Success stories of satisfied customers
- Summaries of recent industry studies or reports
- Survey responses from the last issue

Watch Out!

Newsletters that are designed to be of service to their readers are much more effective marketing tools than those that are mainly promotional pieces. If most of the information in a newsletter is geared toward selling something, it is more likely to be thrown away than be kept and referred to.

- Tips related to the types of products or services the company offers
- Upcoming events

Because the goal of a newsletter is to keep in touch with customers, frequency is important. Quarterly is considered the minimum frequency, with any fewer than four issues per year not enough to keep a customer interested. Certainly, the more frequent your newsletter, the more your customers have cause to think about your business, but that needs to be balanced with the amount of information to be shared and the size of your budget.

Companies that mail a quarterly newsletter often send a larger issue—in terms of number of pages—than those with a monthly or bimonthly newsletter. But if you have a choice between sending a longer issue less frequently or a smaller issue more frequently, always opt for more frequently, no matter what the size of your newsletter.

And although photos and illustrations are nice to have, the most important part of your newsletter is the information it contains. Newsletters that are successful include material that is of interest and relevant to the recipients. Otherwise, it's a waste of time and money.

Case studies

Nearly every type of business has stories to tell about its customers—stories of the success customers have had using its product, following its advice, or implementing its recommendations. You simply gather facts and quotes and write them into stories. Called *case studies*, or *success stories*, these true tales inspire

Money Saver

If your customers are regular users of technology and are comfortable receiving information via e-mail, consider converting your newsletter to electronic format and eliminate the cost to print and mail it. You may still want to have it professionally designed, but your production and distribution costs should drop to zero. You just need a decent customer e-mail list to get started. See Chapter 10.

others to buy from you. They are powerful testimonials that can help convince other customers to buy from you, too.

Finding good case studies

The first step is to identify customers who have benefited from working with your company. Contact each and ask whether he or she is willing to be featured in a case study you're writing up. Interview those who are willing, to better understand exactly how they or their companies changed as a result of buying from you. In addition to a print version, you can also record such interviews and use them as audio files on your Web site or as a separate CD.

Describing the situation

Typically, such stories start with a description of the situation before your company was consulted or your product introduced. After the background is provided, the story of how your company was selected to help solve the problem is told, along with details regarding the implementation process.

So if you run a public relations firm, for example, a case study for one of your clients would describe exactly what you did to overcome the company's problem, including any press materials you may have created, media phone calls you may have made, or opportunities you may have uncovered. Or if you run a health facility, case studies of your clients might describe the different training and exercise regimens you prescribed, along with quotes from your clients about how easy or hard the workouts were.

Noting results and impact

After the change process is covered, you describe what happened next. What positive impact did your company have on your customer? What impressive results were achieved? Quantify those results whenever possible for maximum impact: Number of pounds lost, dollar value of new business obtained, or percent savings achieved are examples of the types of facts and figures potential customers like to read about.

Writing the best case studies

Some tips for creating compelling and interesting case studies are as follows:

- Look for companies in which a change was significant.
- Include quotes from those involved for credibility.
- Weave in as many details as possible—generalities do you no good.
- Make sure the write-up flows logically from beginning to end, although it doesn't necessarily have to be written chronologically.
- Include a relevant photo of the client, the product in use, or the company's facilities to add interest.

After you're satisfied that you've written the story well, send it to your customers to have them read, correct, and approve each case study. The last thing you want to do is to irritate a happy customer by using their information without their permission.

Using your case studies

Case studies are excellent documents to enclose with press kits, but there are plenty of other uses:

- On your Web site
- In your newsletter
- In a direct mail flyer
- As its own direct mailer, when laid out nicely with a photo or two of your customer(s)

Bright Idea

When getting your business cards or brochures printed, have some of your logos printed up on adhesive paper, in various sizes. Then you can place them on plain folders, instead of having folders custom-printed, as well as on other pieces as needed.

- In a brochure
- In an advertisement

Pass along your case studies to your Web designer, your graphic designer, and anyone else who is helping you create your marketing literature to gauge how it can best be used to highlight the benefits of doing business with your company.

Brochures

Some companies don't need a brochure. They get by with a personal meeting, a quote or estimate, and rely on their Web site information to satisfy clients. For some, this works just fine. As people become more reliant on the Internet for information, printed brochures may become less and less important. But even today, being able to hand potential customers an attractive printed brochure that they can take home and review gives you a leg up over all the other companies that didn't make that same investment. However, before you make such an investment, make sure you really need one. If you have few opportunities to give them out, refer potential customers to your Web site, where they can learn all they need about your business.

On the other hand, don't try to cobble a brochure together. A brochure can have a negative impact on your company if it's poorly designed and produced. Brochures that scream home-made or that contain obvious grammar goofs, include mis-spellings, or are unattractive may suggest to some customers that you thought this level of quality was acceptable. A bad brochure can scare customers off.

To avoid this situation, hire a professional graphic designer whose work you like to design your brochure. Ask colleagues for recommendations and look through the designer's portfolio to see whether you spot brochures that you'd be proud to have as your own. Ask for the names of clients they've worked with. Then choose one and forge ahead after you've received an estimate you believe is fair.

Your brochure can be any size you like, with any number of pages stapled or stitched in. In selecting the best format to tell your company's story, consider the number of photos or illustrations you want to include, how much text you feel is important, and what size envelope you want it to fit in. The more unusual the brochure size, the better the chance you'll need to also create a custom-sized envelope to mail it in, which can get pricey.

If you're at a loss as to what information should appear in your brochure, think about:

- Your company's history
- Your products or services
- Benefits of buying from your company
- What makes your business different from the competition
- Your employees' capabilities, skills, or accomplishments
- A list of major customers
- Honors or awards the company has received
- Testimonials
- Case studies or success stories

 Money Saver

When creating printed pieces, be aware that the later in the process you make changes or corrections, the more expensive it gets. Changing the text in your brochure before it's delivered to the printer should cost very little, if anything, but after the printer creates a "blue line" or rough draft of your printed piece, the price to move things around goes up substantially.

Depending on how much space you have available in your brochure, you may not be able to address everything on this list, so hit the high points—the most important facts and noteworthy features. If you're having trouble getting started, turn the task of writing the brochure to a freelance writer. You'll get it done faster with more eloquent results. Then run a draft by some of your best customers to get their reaction. Does it accurately reflect how they view your business? If not, find out what's missing and revise it before going to print.

Folders

Designers I recently spoke with report that folders have become one of the most-requested items for small businesses. In some cases, pocket folders are replacing brochures—the folders are being filled with individual sheets of paper that can be easily and inexpensively updated, if need be. Each page is devoted to one particular aspect of the company's operations, such as its products or services, its history, testimonials, clients, and so on.

In addition to serving as a brochure stand-in, on a temporary or permanent basis, folders can also be used as

■ Press kits

■ Information packets for job applicants or awards applications

■ Covers for quotes and estimates

■ Carryalls for product sell sheets or flyers

■ Holders of presentation handouts

There are certainly many more potential uses of pocket folders emblazoned with your company's name or logo, so don't be limited by these. But consider having some folders printed up if you foresee a need for any of the preceding types of materials.

Posters or calendars

Many companies decide at some point to create promotional giveaways to send to their customers and potential customers. These freebies are generally meant to remind customers of your company's existence, rather than to sell them something, such as a direct mailer attempts to do. See Chapter 15 for more on promotional products.

Some of the most effective printed promotional tools I've seen are posters and calendars. The reason they're so effective is that their design encourages customers to put them near their desk or on the wall in plain sight. Calendars are common promotional items, often sent along with a holiday greeting at the end of the year. The best ones, from a marketing perspective, are those that are attractive without being too sales-y, but that remind the recipient where they came from.

One of the best printed giveaways I've ever seen was a large poster that a division of Kodak used to create every year for its customers. The large image in the background was a scene in nature, such as ripples in sand or blades of grass, and down in one corner was a 12-month calendar. On the opposite corner was the company's logo. Very simple.

Because they were beautiful to look at and large in size, without being heavily promotional, the posters were an extremely popular item. Customers would even call and request them at the end of each year, concerned that they wouldn't receive a replacement for the coming year. That's the kind of reaction you want to have to your materials—people calling to request them, eager to put them up to help promote your company.

Direct mail

Many companies find targeted *direct mailings* (that is, marketing literature with a specific message mailed to people matching very specific criteria) to be the best way to promote their companies. Virtually any printed item sent directly to an individual via the mail qualifies as direct mail, including postcards, flyers, information packets, product samples, and CDs, to name just a few.

With direct mail, the mailing list to which the material is being sent is the most important element. The first step is finding an up-to-date list of potential customers who meet certain specifications, such as home ownership, children under the age of six in the household, or experience buying and selling stocks, or, on the business-to-business side, individuals with decision-making power who work in departments that use your company's products or services.

After the list has been identified or compiled by a mailing list house, you can design a marketing piece that appeals to that particular market's needs and interests. The offer—the enticement designed to encourage someone to commit to a purchase—can make or break a direct mail campaign. The more you know about your target audience, the better able you are to develop an offer that will appeal to them, whether it's a coupon worth 30 percent off one item, a free spa treatment, or a Montblanc pen.

Keep in mind that the value of the offer should be in direct proportion to the request you are making of the recipient. So if you're asking a busy senior executive for a meeting, for example, you'll want to make the offer significant in recognition that you're asking for a major favor. Of if you're trying to entice a couple to make reservations for a luxury cruise this summer, you'll want to offer something more than a free manicure on-board, such as an upgrade to a deck-level suite or free airfare. On the other hand, trying to get people to try a new pack of gum may require only that you give them a coupon for a few cents off.

No matter what the offer, however, consider how you package it. Direct mail specialists report that direct mail campaigns with the highest response rates often use dimensional mail, or a direct mail package that is an odd shape. Boxes, tubes, or oversized packages are most likely to be opened, because the recipient is curious about what could be inside. Similarly, information sent via Priority or overnight mail is also more likely to be opened, especially in an office setting.

When planning your own direct mail campaign, take a close look at your mailing list, your offer, and the design of the piece you're sending to be sure it at least gets opened—that's your biggest challenge of all.

Point-of-purchase displays

For some types of businesses, display units that draw customers' attention to particular products can help boost sales. Used heavily in retail settings, such as at the end of aisles or near the cash register or checkout lane, point-of-purchase (POP) displays encourage impulse buys.

Most wholesalers provide retailers with POP displays in the hopes of landing more real estate in the store for their products. But if you're a wholesaler or distributor, you may want to first discuss POP displays with your retail accounts to see whether they would make room if you were to provide POPs. And if you're a retailer, you may want to request them, or design your own to bring attention to a certain category of product that has the potential to move quickly if showcased properly, such as seasonal merchandise.

Work with a firm that specializes in creating such displays, as well as consulting your customers to determine what size and shape of display will best meet their needs. The worst thing you can do is to design a beautiful POP display that your retailers won't use or customers won't notice—that's just money down the drain.

Catalogs

Another effective marketing tool used by retailers, industrial product manufacturers, wholesalers, and mail order operations, to name a few, is a product catalog. Most people receive some type of catalog at least once a week, from office supply stores, clothing retailers, home furnishings companies, toy sellers, and many others. Catalogs are often effective because they showcase a wide selection of products and are sent to households or business owners who have a history of buying such products, or who have shown at least an interest.

Bright Idea

If you don't have enough consumer products to warrant creating your own catalog, consider trying to get your products included in other companies' catalogs. A good resource to identify possible catalog partners is the *National Directory of Catalogs.*

Unfortunately, catalogs are extremely expensive to produce—expect to invest at least $10,000 for such a tool. Even on a small scale, the cost to design the piece, photograph the products, print, and mail it is exorbitant. A more cost-effective solution is to direct customers to an online catalog. Take a look at Chapter 10 for more information about this.

Just the facts

- Hiring a professional graphic designer to create your marketing materials ensures you have tools that reflect your company's desired image and reputation.

- Basic printed pieces that every small business should have include business cards with complementary letterhead, envelopes, and mailing labels.

- Other pieces of marketing literature that can be helpful in attracting new customers and educating existing customers about the range of products and services you offer are note cards, newsletters, case studies, brochures and folders, posters and calendars, direct mail pieces, a product catalog, and point-of-purchase displays.

- To get the most out of your investment in printed marketing materials, find ways to use them several times during the year, rather than just once or twice.

Chapter 12

GET THE SCOOP ON...
Finding three ways to sell more ■ Enticing customers back ■ Attracting new customers ■
Creating effective incentive programs ■ Doing
more business with current customers

Sales Promotion Opportunities

To build your business—or even just to stay in business—you need to sell your products or services to customers. The more you sell, the more money you make, assuming your offerings are priced profitably. However, there are only three basic ways to grow your business and make more money:

- Find new customers
- Sell greater quantities of products of services to your existing customers
- Sell new or higher value products or services to your existing customers

Although most businesses spend a good portion of their marketing budget trying to attract new customers, you'll notice that only one of the three approaches involves finding new customers. Finding and convincing new customers to buy from you is actually much more costly and difficult than encouraging people who have already bought from you to buy more or to buy additional items. This explains why

two of the three growth methods focus on existing customers—
people who are likely to buy from you again and may need very
little prodding to do so.

Whether your goal is to broaden your customer base by
attracting new buyers or to increase sales by enticing your current customers to buy more from you, there are a number of
marketing methods you can use.

Categorized as sales promotion tools, these marketing tactics
all aim to generate sales. Some require considerable time and
planning, while others are fairly simple to design and execute.
All have the potential to generate significant growth.

Selling to new customers

According to the author of the *Loyalty Effect,* it costs five times
more to establish a new customer relationship than to keep an
existing one, suggesting that pursuing new customers is costly. It
is, but new businesses or companies that have undergone significant change need to focus their marketing on attracting new
customers because there are too few existing customers on
which to base a business. Fortunately, there are a number of
proven marketing tactics to drum up new business.

Giving them a taste: Sampling

One of the best promotional techniques involves giving potential
customers firsthand experience with your company's products or
services through a sample. Letting them see for themselves exactly
how your product or service can benefit them can convert
potential buyers to paying customers relatively quickly, depending on your normal sales cycle. That is, if it frequently takes
12 months or more to secure a deal, sampling may help shave
that to 10 or 11 months. But if your product is an impulse purchase, you may be able to land some new customers on the spot,
as many grocery stores do with their in-store sampling program.

Offering small samples of food has become commonplace at
grocery stores nationwide, where food manufacturers set up

tables at the end of aisles, complete with tasty morsels available to shoppers. Sometimes, the samples are right out of the box, such as with drinks or crackers, and other times, they may be an ingredient in prepared dishes, such as meats or dip mixes, that are served in little cups or on plates. It is the manufacturer's hope that people who have never tried their product before will get the chance, and then decide to purchase the product for use at home.

The same is true at KrispyKreme doughnut stores, where an original glazed doughnut is offered to everyone in line.

Although sampling works very well with products, it is also an effective tool in the service industry. Some cable companies, for example, offer a free month of digital video recorder (DVR) service to customers who are interested in trying the technology. After 30 days, customers can either start paying the monthly fee or return the DVR box and owe nothing. With no upfront cost, such deals are a great way to entice consumers to try something new, with little or no risk to them.

By the same token, sampling is just as effective in the business-to-business world. Some advertising agencies will offer to prepare a set of advertisements for a potential new client—generally with a hefty budget—to review, at no cost, in the hopes of wowing them and winning their future business. On the manufacturing side, suppliers may offer product samples or prepare prototypes to demonstrate their capabilities, as a way for potential clients to sample their expertise. Interactive game developers will also produce a small sample to demonstrate their animation capabilities to potential clients at no cost.

 Money Saver

If you buy products from a distributor or wholesaler, ask whether they can provide you with samples. You may be able to buy them at a discount, or get some for free, by asking.

Sampling is smart, though it can be rather expensive for small businesses on a large scale. To keep costs under control, consider creating a prioritized list of target clients for whom you are willing to prepare samples, or determine the maximum number of samples you can afford to give away before implementing such a program.

Other companies use samples as purchase incentives, versus giveaways, thereby ensuring that some money will be made for each sample distributed. Cosmetic company Estee Lauder's Clinique brand is a pioneer in sampling, having virtually created the promotional concept for its industry. Several times a year, Clinique schedules "Bonus Time," which are days when customers receive a package of several product samples with every purchase over a certain dollar value. The Clinique cosmetic counters are almost always mobbed during these times, and Clinique successfully introduces its customers to new products with each free gift.

Pairing new product samples with product purchases is a smart way to encourage sales while laying the groundwork for future sales of the sampled goods. Partnering with other companies is another savvy move.

Co-operative classics

Co-operative marketing, including sales promotion, is a low-cost means of introducing your business to potential customers through an organization with which they already have a relationship. Sure, you could send out a direct mail flyer or letter inviting them to do business with you on your own, but a flyer or letter from a company where they already do business is more likely to get opened, read, and acted on.

 Watch Out!

Some companies may ask you to prepare a sample of your work *on spec,* which means "on speculation" and is common in the marketing industry. On spec means you'll only be paid for your work if they decide to retain your services, which doesn't happen often. Be aware of your odds before you say "yes."

To expand your list of potential customers, make a list of businesses that are potential marketing partners. These could include

- Businesses in your immediate area, such as your building, shopping plaza, or town
- Businesses that provide complementary products and services—offerings that work well with yours, but don't compete, such as repair services or consulting firms dealing in your particular type of product
- Businesses targeting your same audience, such as new moms or major corporations
- Businesses that sell your same products and services, but in different parts of town, such as consignment shops or restaurants
- Businesses that belong to the same trade organization or networking group, including Business Networking International or the Young Entrepreneurs Organization, for example

Next, consider how you'd like to structure your relationship. Do you merely want to swap mailing lists and do your own individual marketing campaigns? Do you want to pool your resources and approach both your customer bases together? Are you willing to make a promotional offer to their customers or to provide an endorsement of the other business to your customers?

Before agreeing to join forces with another business (or businesses), be sure to check them out first. What is their reputation? What kinds of customers do they have—are customers too different from yours to be worth marketing to? How is their customer service? What are their marketing goals?

Because you are effectively aligning your business with another, take precautions to protect your business. Early on, it would be wise to tread carefully. Start by trading mailing lists, for example, with no further obligation. Then, if all seems to go well, brainstorm other ways you could work together.

Another approach is to offer to partner with other, generally complementary, businesses. Together, you could create a mailer to be sent to their customers with a special offer. For example, in the bridal industry, a wine retailer could partner with a local jeweler and mail a letter to their customers to say that because they bought their rings from your jeweler colleague, you'd like to give them a free bottle of champagne. All they need to do is come in and introduce themselves.

Similarly, a caterer could partner with a wedding photographer and offer a free petite cake to the photographer's bridal clients, or the photographer could offer a free engagement photo to couples who haven't already selected a photographer for their big day.

In these cases, the potential customers have already been qualified as potentially needing wedding-related services in the near future, thereby increasing the odds that a marketing campaign to them will result in a sale.

Such cooperative campaigns can be very cost-effective, especially if you agree to share or exchange mailing lists for free. And if you agree to share the cost of producing any mailers or literature, your costs can drop even further.

Partnering can be very effective, whether the other organization is a business or a charity. In fact, partnering with a charity may be even more effective.

Partnering with a nonprofit

If your target customer is the member of a particular nonprofit organization or charity, partnering with that organization can be an especially effective means of gaining an introduction to their supporters. For example, a pet supply store could support the local SPCA or a bookstore could partner with a literacy organization.

Most nonprofit organizations hold major fundraising events, such as gala dinners, auctions, fashion shows, and wine tastings, to name just a few. Such special events are months in

Bright Idea

If you have a location that customers visit, ask some of your clients whether they would be willing to write a short letter or testimonial on their letterhead that you could hang in your entryway or foyer. Then have these letters nicely framed and hung. You'll gain credibility, and they'll gain free advertising.

If you're not already getting referrals, there are a number of marketing methods you can use to encourage them.

Make sure current customers are happy

First, you need to be sure your current customers are happy with you. Are they satisfied with the services they've been receiving? Is there anything that bothers them? Are the products they've bought meeting their needs? Before you start pursuing referrals, make sure your current customers are delighted.

Let customers know that you want referrals

Second, let your customers know that you are trying to expand your business and would welcome referrals from them. You can do this a number of ways:

- Casually mention during a conversation with customers that your XYZ part of the business is booming, but that you'd welcome suggestions from them on other customers who might also need those services. This works best in high-end and business-to-business industries.

- Offer a reward for each new customer referred, such as a free product, discount on future work you'll perform, a gift certificate, or free service. This works well in personal service businesses.

- Send a letter that describes your plans for growth and ask for help in identifying new customers. Enclose a form that can be faxed or mailed back with the names and contact information of likely candidates. This works especially well in business-to-business settings.

- Schedule a special event for customers and their friends, during which both will receive a percentage off any purchases, which encourages customers to bring along their pals. Retailers and direct marketers do well with these types of events.

Distributing coupons

A final way to boost sales to new customers is to offer a promotional coupon to encourage a first purchase. Consumer product manufacturers do this day in and day out with cents-off coupons distributed in Sunday newspapers, and major retailers are forever offering percentage-off deals, so why shouldn't you? Be sure that the discount offer is substantial enough to interest your customers and is not insulting, such as fifty cents off a $100 purchase.

One way to ensure that coupons don't lose you money is to be specific about which products or services they can be applied to. Perhaps you'll give a percentage off, but only on regularly priced merchandise. Or maybe you'll honor a coupon, but only on purchases over $100, or on weekdays. You can specify when coupons are valid to reduce any potential loss on your end, but be careful about becoming too restrictive. Coupons that are hard to redeem will be less effective at drawing in new customers, and that's your primary objective.

Some common and lesser-known places to distribute coupons include the following:

- Newspaper inserts
- ValPak and other monthly mailing programs
- Your Web site

 Watch Out!

When partnering with a nonprofit, keep in mind that the organization is not another business. Don't go overboard in asking for benefits in exchange for your participation. As a charity, it's best to err on the side of being generous with your time, if not your money, rather than seem uncaring or stingy.

Bright Idea

In addition to attracting new customers, coupons are also a good way of tracking where your new business is coming from. Add a code to each coupon so you can tell where, and perhaps when, it originated.

- Local Web sites
- Church or synagogue newsletters
- School newsletters
- Bill stuffers
- Paycheck stuffers at area companies
- Hotels and restaurants
- Community bulletin boards

Although the perception is that coupon users are skinflints, demographics from the Coupon Industry Council suggests that, in fact, coupon users are quite upscale. But coupons are generally best for consumer purchases or smaller business needs, such as office supplies, rather than multimillion dollar computer systems and strategic consulting. Offering a coupon for a percentage off a $5 million business-to-business deal could damage your firm's credibility. To be safe, limit coupons to business-to-consumer offerings.

Selling more to existing customers

Although expanding your customer base by attracting new customers is gratifying, it's not the best use of your marketing dollars. In fact, the Small Business Administration cites a statistic from the Customer Service Institute that 65 percent of a company's business is from existing customers. Using that as a rough guideline, approximately 65 percent—the majority—of your marketing budget and effort should be devoted to doing more business with your current customers.

The main differences between marketing to new customers and existing ones is that with new customers, you frequently need to blanket your local market to determine who is a likely buyer. Marketing to everyone in the hopes of attracting a subset of buyers is rather wasteful, which is why it's always better to market to a group of people who have already bought from you. You know where they work or where they live, and you have their addresses, phone numbers, and e-mail addresses. And the likelihood that your message will be received and read is also higher with existing customers.

Another difference is that new customers may not have heard of your company or be aware of your services, so you need to spend more time, or space, in your marketing just educating them about who you are and what you offer. Existing customers, on the other hand, have already done business with you, so you need only to remind them that you're still there, still ready to serve them.

Assuming the majority of your customers are satisfied and would do business with you again, your marketing should yield a decent return on investment every time you make contact with your existing customers. That is, every direct mailer you send should translate into new business from your customers. Every e-zine you distribute to your customers should prompt a percentage of them to make contact and buy from you again. And every promotional offer should entice at least a few of them to take you up on your offer.

Initiating a frequent buyer program

One of the best ways to make your customers even more loyal to your business is to create a frequent buyer program that rewards customers for the purchases they make from you; the more they buy, the more rewards they qualify for. And all things being equal, they're more likely to buy from you than another company in order to earn some rewards.

The classic example of a frequent buyer program is airline frequent flyer miles, where airline passengers receive reward points for every mile flown on a particular airline. But even small retailers can establish a frequent buyer program to reward their best customers for their increased patronage.

Restaurants also have rewards programs that entitle regular patrons to free meals, as do tanning salons, garden shops, bookstores, and beauty salons, to name a few.

On the business-to-business side, some wholesalers and distributors reward their biggest accounts—those companies that buy the most from them—with trips, deep discounts, complimentary conference or trade show attendance, and bonus *co-op advertising*, in which the company chips in a certain percentage of an advertisement's cost in exchange for mentioning their product in the ad.

The best frequent buyer programs are communicated to all customers, with clear information about how rewards are earned and redeemed and what rewards are available. Reminders about qualifying for rewards also go a long way toward keeping your company and potential rewards in the customer's mind, which is right where you want to be.

Some companies use special software designed to track each customer's purchases, such as women's clothier Chico's, which uses a Passport card to identify regular customers. Customers who have purchased enough to qualify for a reward earn a percentage off each purchase when they present their plastic ID cards.

A potential downside of frequent buyer programs is that customers get hooked, and it's hard to shut them down later, as the airlines are now finding out. But if the program is working, bringing customers in more frequently for purchases, then presumably, there would be no reason to eliminate it.

Holding special on-site events

In stark contrast to ongoing methods of encouraging purchases, special events are one-time or several-times-a-year occurrences designed to drive up sales. Used frequently in retail environments, such short-lived events give customers another reason to come into the store on a particular day. From the retailer's perspective, not only does it encourage sales, but special events can also reconnect a customer to the company.

Major mall department stores sometimes hold midnight madness sales, during which store hours are extended to allow customers to shop later, often with special promotions during the late-night hours. Early morning sales on black Friday (the day after Thanksgiving) are the same type of event, just at a different hour of the day. Other variations of such an event include a teen night, usually on a Friday or Saturday night, when teenagers are invited to shop and receive services just for them. Spas and boutiques have found this tactic works particularly well, especially when pizza is promised. Holding a benefit event, staying open late on a Sunday afternoon, or donating a percentage of the event's sales to a particular charity are all other special events that work well.

Art galleries or gift shops can hold an open house and invite artisans whose works are on display to demonstrate their creative technique. A music store or piano seller could invite a musician in for a free concert or give a free lesson to new students.

In some cases, it matters less what the theme or reason for the sale is, as long as some criteria are met, such as providing childcare. One consignment store in upstate New York holds semiannual Mom's night out events, during which an in-store babysitter is provided to watch young children while Mom shops and enjoys light hors d'oeuvres.

To brainstorm ideas for a special event you could hold, consider your target audience, when they frequently shop (or would prefer to shop), and what kinds of interests they have.

Would they be more likely to come and shop to take advantage of a great special sale, or would the promise of a dessert buffet provided by a local caterer be a bigger draw? Do they enjoy mingling with authors and artists, or would they prefer a demonstration or class? What would appeal most to your customers?

If you can't answer that question, you may want to ask your customers themselves. Set up a simple one-question survey on your Web site, by your cash register, or in your newsletter, for example, and ask what kind of special event would be most exciting to them. If you have some ideas and would like some feedback, list those and ask your customers to rank them in order of interest. After you've zeroed in on a theme you think will work, start planning.

Selling higher value offerings to existing customers

If your customers are already buying regularly from you, it may be easier to upgrade them to more expensive offerings than to convince them to buy more frequently. That's essentially the strategy that many grocery stores are taking. Given that there is only so much milk, chicken, and eggs we can all eat in a week, there comes a point at which it's tough to increase the frequency of consumer purchases. However, adding more upscale products, such as convenience foods, is increasing the value of the checkout total. Higher value products, where more labor has been invested to ready them for eating—such as washed and chopped vegetables or complete gourmet dinners—command a higher price point that many busy families are willing to pay. They may shop at the grocery store the same number of times each week, but by adding more expensive convenience items to their basket, the amount spent is climbing.

Increasing the total amount customers spend with you each year, or each purchase, is a third strategy for making more money in your business.

Your customers already know you, already love you, and are already buying regularly from you, but the key is to encourage them to try new products and services that are more expensive than what they are currently enjoying. Blockbuster's new monthly rental option is an example of this strategy, where infrequent movie renters, who might have spent $5 or $10 a month, are being converted to an unlimited monthly rental program that costs around $15 a month. That's $5 more a month, or $60 more a year, per customer that Blockbuster can now earn.

The biggest challenge, of course, is convincing the customer to try something new. Fortunately, there are some strategies to overcome that potential reluctance or nervousness.

Giving a guarantee

One of the best ways to encourage a customer to try something new is to offer an unconditional guarantee. Promising your customers that, if they aren't happy with the new product or service, you'll refund their money removes all their risk and makes them more open to considering a change. This tactic is especially effective with expensive services, such as management consulting fees, Web site designs, or luxury automobiles, where the customer may be nervous about committing a sizeable chunk of money; providing a guarantee lessens that nervousness and may move your company and its offerings to the top choice. But it also works with less expensive products, such as makeup, as Rite Aid's money-back guarantee suggests.

Interestingly, although buyers factor a guarantee into the purchase decision, very few actually make a return. That is, studies have shown that offering a guarantee is much more likely to make you money than to cost you money, because it increases the odds that someone will make a purchase without increasing the odds that they will ultimately invoke the guarantee. Plus, most small businesses stand behind their products and services anyway. If that's the case at your company, why not make it part of your marketing message.

Giving rebates

A similar tactic to encourage sales, especially involving upgrades, is to offer a rebate. *Rebates* are refunds made to buyers who submit proof of having made the purchase, plus any other qualifying materials the manufacturer requests. Although refunds have been commonly used by consumer product manufacturers for years, other marketers are now getting into the act. You've probably noticed office product companies, appliance manufacturers, and auto dealers using rebates, too.

Like guarantees, rebates encourage buyers to favor one product over another. The main difference is that rebates emphasize price as an important factor in the purchase decision, by offering money back. However, rebates also have a low redemption rate—currently around 21 percent, according to the Promotion Marketing Association—making it another example of a marketing method that can boost sales without significantly raising costs.

When structuring a rebate offer, be clear about what is required to qualify for the money back. Making it too complicated, however, will make it less likely that buyers will complete it, and less likely that it will be a factor in their decision making. That is, don't waste your time creating a rebate offer if your intent is to discourage customers from actually filling it out. But do set an expiration date for the rebate program to push customers to make a decision sooner rather than later.

Offering discounts

Whereas rebates offer money back following a purchase, a *discount* is an up-front price reduction that shrinks the buyer's cash outlay. For that reason, they can be a powerful promotional tool. They're also another means of encouraging customers to choose one product over another. In fact, the presence of a discount can push customers to buy a more expensive product.

Watch Out!

Before offering a discount, be sure that your product's or service's profit margins can support it. You may end up selling more, but lose money because the discount exceeded your profit margin.

Discount offers can be structured to encourage higher sales of particular categories of products or services—rather than simply discounting all your offerings across the board—and can be on a sliding scale, increasing as the total value of the sale climbs.

Just the facts

- There are three primary ways to increase your sales: find new customers; sell a greater quantity to your existing customer base; and sell higher value offerings to your existing customers.

- New customers may need to be given a reason to do business with you, because they may be pleased with their current suppliers.

- Increasing the amount of business you do with existing customers can be facilitated with a frequent buyer program or special events.

- Convincing your customers to upgrade to a more expensive product or service can be accomplished with the help of money-back guarantees, rebates, and discounts.

In-Person Marketing

Many companies today appear to be putting a high priority on marketing efficiency—reaching the most customers in the least time to generate the most business—rather than customer relationship building. The focus has shifted to increasing the number of sales transactions, rather than building lifetime customers. Certainly that's not true in every case, but many businesses seem to be investing in marketing tools that enable them to fulfill customer needs with the least amount of human interaction possible. That's dangerous.

Potential customers today are frequently referred to a Web site for more information, where they can submit questions via e-mail or skim a list of online FAQs (frequently asked questions) to find answers. Many companies purposely bury their phone number within the Web site, or leave it off altogether, so as to reduce the need for live phone operators. Most consumers don't mind this self-service mentality, but what they fail to develop is an emotional connection to the company. That's where companies that make an effort to connect face to face with customers have

Chapter 13

a distinct advantage. It's an advantage you may want to build into your own marketing efforts.

That's not to say that you should attempt to meet with each and every potential customer—it's not feasible or always worth the time—but you may want to look for focused opportunities to network with qualified customers. Trade shows are an excellent start.

Manning a booth at trade shows

Because of their size and scope, trade shows, expos, and industry conferences are generally very efficient ways to network with potential customers, suppliers, and potential referral sources all in one place. No need for you to fly around the country for individual meetings—you can catch many important contacts at trade shows, where they've traveled at their expense.

Some companies pay to set up booths when there is exhibition space and erect displays to educate their target audience about what they have to offer. If you're a manufacturer or distributor and have products to sell, this can be very effective—product demonstrations can really drive home your product's advantages better than any other type of presentation. The cost can be rather steep, depending on the show, but given the number of prospects you could come in contact with, it may be well worth the investment.

If you're a business-to-business service provider, a booth can still be worth the expense, but you may find that registering to attend the show can work just as well, at a much lower cost. The difference is that instead of coming to you, you walk booth to booth to introduce yourself to exhibitors who are also

---

 Bright Idea

Bring along a camera to take photos of customers and prospects that you can use in a customer newsletter. If you're permitted, you may also want to take pictures of competitors' booths to get ideas for improving your own.

prospects. The major disadvantage is if a booth is busy, or one of the exhibitor's potential customers comes along, the company you're trying to get to know may push you aside. However, there are some ways of getting around that.

Some companies, instead of registering for a display booth on the trade show floor, will reserve a conference room or meeting room elsewhere in the hotel or convention center, where they schedule meetings throughout the day with their potential customers. That way, they can take advantage of their prospects having already paid all their own transportation expenses, but still get some one-on-one time to talk about working together. Whether you spring for the exhibition space or decide instead to register and walk the show, there are a number of ways you may be able to get more bang for your marketing buck at the show. Here are some ideas:

- If you reserve booth space, inquire about any opportunities to lead a seminar during the educational portion of the conference, which most shows offer.

- If you are approached about speaking at a show, request free admission to the event in exchange, as well as booth space and a list of attendees. Not every show organizer can give it, but some will if you ask.

- Mail out invitations mentioning an incentive for prospects to stop by your booth while at the show. The incentive could be a giveaway, such as a free report or a handy iPod accessory, or a raffle for a nice prize, such as a restaurant gift certificate or high-tech gizmo.

- Offer to write an article for any show bulletins or guides in exchange for a byline.

- Ask the organizer about any opportunities to market to registered participants in their hotel rooms—maybe promotional material inside their morning newspaper or along with show information.

Watch Out!

There is a thin line between persistence and stalking, so be careful to stay on the correct side. No response from a prospect should generally be interpreted as "I'm not interested." That doesn't mean you should give up entirely, but back off a bit, lest you come off as seeming desperate.

Trade shows are excellent places for one-on-one interaction and networking with large numbers of people, but if your target customer list consists of far fewer numbers, you may want to set your sights on a few in-person meetings at the customers' homes or businesses.

Setting up appointments and meetings

Although retailers and restaurants generally spend their marketing dollars to encourage customers to come to them, if you're a service provider, manufacturer, wholesaler, or other type of business, you may need to go to your customers to persuade them to do business with you. That entails convincing prospects to spend some time with you during an initial appointment or meeting.

Some companies prefer to *cold call* prospects, placing a phone call to potential customers who may have never had any contact with the business, to request a few minutes of their time. Although most consumers today consider such calls intrusive, business professionals generally consider it part of their jobs and may be willing to spend a little time with you.

Other companies prefer to introduce themselves by way of an introductory package of information, and then follow up by phone to get an appointment, which is generally called a *warm call,* which you can hear much more about in Chapter 14.

Such appointments are an important step toward winning a customer's business, because it is your chance to get to know them, to learn about their needs and preferences, and to demonstrate why your business is the one best equipped to provide needed services. Whether you're a financial planner in pursuit of new advisory clients, an ad agency interested in working with a major local corporation, or a construction firm eager to bid on upcoming city projects, the best way to get the ball rolling on any project is to set up a face-to-face meeting.

Of course, it generally isn't this easy: You dial the phone, and get connected to your prospect, who eagerly agrees to spend half an hour with you. More likely, you'll call several times, leave a message on voicemail or with a secretary explaining the reason for your call, and never hear back. Don't take it personally. But do brainstorm other ways you can come into contact with that individual, in the hopes of securing that coveted meeting.

Networking with colleagues and friends to find out if anyone knows your prospect is a great first step. Googling the individual to find out about any nonprofit organizations they belong to, or boards they sit on, is another way to try to find possible connections.

But be persistent and check in once in a while, perhaps mailing articles or studies you find that you think your prospect may be interested in, as you see them. Stay in touch once a quarter until you get some positive response to your attempts at contact.

After you land an appointment, make the most of it by being fully prepared. Ask your key contact about the types of audiovisual aids that may be available in the room where you'll be presenting. There's nothing worse than arriving with overhead cells, only to learn they were expecting you'd be using PowerPoint, or vice versa. And pay close attention to what you see and hear—note your prospect's body language and nonverbal clues regarding what is of greatest interest and concern, as well as what he or she has to say.

 Bright Idea

Find out whether there will be a press room for media representatives, and if so, make sure there are plenty of press kits about your firm available there. You may need to drop them off yourself, but it's worth the effort.

Making presentations

If your initial meeting goes well with a prospect, you may eventually earn the opportunity to make a presentation to a group of decision makers within the company.

A presentation is your opportunity to make the case for hiring your firm or using your company's products and services. During your presentation, make sure you give enough specifics that the group you are presenting to can make an informed decision, but don't bore them with too much detail. And make sure to leave plenty of time for questions—both for your benefit and theirs.

Hearing their questions and concerns gives you a clue regarding issues you might not have been aware of. For example, you may have spent most of your presentation explaining the reliability of your company's security system believing that was the biggest concern. But if, during the question-and-answer session, you hear a lot of questions about price or service, you now know those are areas your company will be evaluated on.

Although many companies believe the opportunity to make a presentation is mainly for the benefit of the potential customer, it's really an opportunity for both parties to assess whether there is a good business fit. And it's a chance for you to ask questions as well.

When you receive a question from someone in the audience, you might take the opportunity to ask one, too. First respond and answer the question posed, but then ask one of your own, such as "Is that a major concern for XYZ company?" Or, if asked about the time required to complete a project, you might ask, "What is the timeline you were hoping for?"

 Watch Out!

When you knock on someone's door for the first time, it is recommended that you take two or three large steps back, away from the door, so as not to intimidate the person you're trying to sell to. You want to appear helpful, not as a threat.

Bright Idea

It's a good idea to have handouts of your talk, especially if you're making a capabilities presentation or are recommending a particular strategy. This way, attendees can reflect on what you said and compare it to other candidates without having to go on memory alone.

The opportunity to present to a group generally means your company is in serious contention for a project—perhaps even a finalist. Given that, invest extra time to be sure your presentation will knock their socks off.

Presentations aren't appropriate in all circumstances, however, such as business-to-consumer sales, where your prospects are individuals or families and you need to market to them at home. In those instances, door-to-door selling may be a better strategy.

Door-to-door calls

Quite common in the early twentieth century, door-to-door sales are now the exception rather than the rule, but it can be effective, as Girl Scouts selling cookies always find. It can be especially appropriate if you need to see the property in order to provide an estimate, too. For example, if you're a landscaping company, it helps you to see how large the yard is before providing an estimate to do any kind of planting work for the homeowners. Likewise, if you're a lawn service trying to drum up regular lawn-cutting work—you need to see how large the yard is in order to be sure you're quoting a reasonable fee.

Cold calling

Or, if you're a window-washing business, driveway-sealing company, or pet containment business, a visit—even a drive by—can help you more accurately price your services.

And like telemarketing services, one approach is to show up unannounced on a potential customer's doorstep, while another is to mail materials in advance of your visit, in the hopes of spurring the homeowner to give some thought to hiring you.

When you mail materials, be sure and mention that you'll "be in the neighborhood next week and will stop by to discuss the information," or something to that effect. You want to alert your prospect that you'll be dropping by, so that they're more inclined to open the door and talk to you. Some people don't like surprises.

Be on the lookout for signs in the window that indicate "No solicitors," meaning that you are not welcome. In those instances, you'll want to call ahead or make contact beforehand in order to get the go-ahead to ring their doorbell. Otherwise, you won't get anywhere and you may ruin your chances of ever doing business with the person on the other side of the door.

Direct sales

Of course, door-to-door selling is not the only way to show your wares and encourage customers to buy. A better—and very popular—way to do this is to hold a party in your home, or in someone else's home, where you show off your product line, allow the group to see your offerings up close and personal, and encourage them to buy.

Called *direct sales,* this marketing and sales approach is working wonders for companies that sell everything from jewelry (Silpada), gourmet cooking instruments (Pampered Chef), high-end women's clothing (Carlisle), classy home décor (Southern Living), and many others. By recruiting others to host gatherings in their home and invite their circle of friends, you have a prequalified group of prospects to sell to. The incentive for someone to host such a meeting, or party, is free merchandise or a credit toward their purchase.

 Bright Idea

For homes where you're unable to reach someone at home, leave behind a *door hanger*—a printed advertisement that wraps around the door handle letting homeowners know you were there. Providing the information may encourage prospects to call you to get more information.

If you find that interacting with customers one-on-one is your key to success, and you have a product that can be demonstrated or displayed in a small-group setting, direct sales could be a gold mine for you. And the only real marketing tools you need are invitations, which can even be distributed via e-mail by the host or hostess, and order forms.

Using sandwich boards

Other ways to make face-to-face contact with people are with signs and advertisements you wear, or you hire someone to wear. The idea is to get their attention with the information on your sign, which you follow up with witty repartée, or at least a conversation about the product, service, or company mentioned on the board.

Sandwich board advertising is generally more effective when the person wearing it is standing outside a retail store, restaurant, or event, and is challenged with generating interest in coming in. Anything more difficult than that, and sandwich boards are not the best marketing tool. They're a conversation starter of sorts, but they won't make a sale.

Handing out flyers

Another marketing method where face-to-face contact is made is with flyers that you physically hand out, rather than mail. Again, you may decide to try this yourself, but most businesses hire others to distribute flyers. From what I've seen, the most effective at this are people who are warm, friendly, and outspoken.

Of course, this marketing method isn't appropriate for every kind of business, because flyers are generally associated with less expensive items, such as food, tourist activities, and sales. If you're a high-end business or have a high-end clientèle, handing out flyers—even in their neighborhood—is very likely to be a waste of time. But if you've opened a new restaurant, store, or personal service—such as a nail salon or grocery delivery—this could work well.

Some companies opt to put flyers underneath car windshields instead of initiating a personal conversation—I discourage this. Few people take note of what is on the pieces of paper stuffed under their windshields, and the whole point of this tool is to strike up a conversation with a prospect that could lead to a customer relationship. Avoiding any kind of personal contact defeats the purpose of this marketing tool.

Just the facts

- Online marketing can significantly improve your company's marketing efficiency, but at the expense of building relationships with customers that can lead to long-term loyalty and sales. Interacting with customers face to face can significantly increase sales.

- Landing a face-to-face meeting with a business professional prospect can be your ticket to new business opportunities.

- Door-to-door selling has become less popular, but can still work in instances where you need to physically see the location in order to provide a work estimate or recommendations.

- Direct selling, where you or a host or hostess invites a small group of potential customers into your home or office, has proven to be an excellent way to demonstrate products and entice attendees to buy.

- Hiring workers to wear sandwich boards and chat with passers-by can work to bring customers in to a nearby store or restaurant, but isn't as effective elsewhere. The same is true of handing out flyers.

GET THE SCOOP ON...
Dealing with rules and regulations ▪ Discovering
the importance of research ▪ Making effective
cold calls ▪ Encouraging in-bound calls

Telemarketing

With a record 76 percent of American adults having joined the Federal Trade Commission's Do Not Call Registry as of January 2006, three years after it was created, you might think that telemarketing is nearly dead. But you'd be wrong. In fact, the Direct Marketing Association's 2005 Response Rate Report, which provides data regarding the most effective direct marketing methods, found that marketing by telephone was the most effective means of securing orders, as well as for generating a response to an offer, beating out both direct mail and catalogs.

The trick to success with telemarketing is following some smart guidelines for making phone calls, and not getting discouraged by the series of "no's" you're going to hear.

Rules you don't want to break

Because the telephone is so widely used for marketing by businesses small and large, the U.S. Federal Trade Commission (FTC) has developed rules and regulations to protect consumers on the receiving end of such calls—protection mainly from fraud and harassment. A majority of the requirements have to do with truthfulness and with proving that the buyer truly agreed to make a purchase. The rest deal with identifying yourself as a salesperson and limiting the hours of the day calls can be made.

To avoid racking up penalties of $11,000 per transgression, as well as potentially ruining a future customer relationship, you'll want to be aware of the fundamental guidelines of the Telephone Sales Rule, which were updated and amended in 2003. Keep in mind that these rules were made primarily to protect consumers, not businesses, so if you are a business-to-business venture, you are exempt from these regulations unless you are selling "nondurable office or cleaning supplies."

Although reviewing the entire Telephone Sales Rule yourself would be a good idea if you intend to do some telemarketing, the basic guidelines are as follows:

- You may not call anyone on the Do Not Call Registry unless your company has an "established business relationship" with them.

- You must reveal the name of your company, or the company on whose behalf you are calling, through your Caller ID system, as well as your telephone number (you can't block it, that is).

- You must remove any phone number of a consumer from your database if they so request it, such as by asking to be added to your do-not-call list.

- You may only call between the hours of 8:00 a.m. and 9:00 p.m.

- You must keep records regarding advertising and promotional material, sales records, employee records, and authorizations or records of agreement related to your telemarketing efforts for two years.

- You must identify yourself as a representative of the company and state that you're making a sales call.

Watch Out!

It's against the law to call anyone whose name is on the Do Not Call list, unless you have an established business relationship.

- You may not leave out important details about the product or service you are trying to sell, nor can you lie about it.

So if you intend only to call customers in your company's database—meaning they've done business with you already—you may not be required to compare your list with the Do Not Call Registry. However, because past customers with whom you don't have an *ongoing* relationship may be covered by the rule, it would be worth your time to scan the Do Not Call Registry at www.telemarketing.donotcall.gov. At the Web site, you can either download the latest file of numbers that are off-limits or download just the changes to the most recent version—a faster way to check on recently added numbers if you've previously downloaded the entire file.

The cost to access the data is free for the first five area codes you need to check. After that, the cost is $25 per year per area code.

A new rule, as of January 2005, also requires that telemarketers access the registry at least once every 31 days to download the new numbers that have been added to the Do Not Call Registry.

Most of the regulations are of little consequence if you're running a typical small business, but if you intend to try some business-to-consumer selling by telephone, you'll want to bone up on the specific rules to avoid getting a hefty fine.

Whether you're calling a consumer or business, there are some generally accepted processes that successful telemarketers use to boost their results—processes you can easily develop and employ in your own business.

Bright Idea

Any questions about the Federal Trade Commission's regulations regarding telemarketing calls can probably be answered by reviewing a booklet on the subject, produced by the Direct Marketing Association, which is available at www.the-dma.org/telemarketing/tsr_compliance_guide.pdf.

Cold calling

Telemarketing has been around nearly as long as the telephone has existed, and yet few of us have ever grown accustomed to, or comfortable with, making *cold calls*. Having to pick up the phone and call someone you don't know, someone who may be averse to speaking with you, can be daunting. Yet successful entrepreneurs frequently cite cold calling as the secret to their success, presumably because so few of their competitors are doing it.

What differentiates the successful cold caller is preparation: researching your prospective customer, developing a script to guide the conversation (or at least what you'll say), and clarifying exactly what you hope to gain by making the call (an appointment). Your objective in making a cold call isn't always to make an immediate sale. In some cases, it's to schedule a time to sit down with your prospect to reveal how you can help them, whether your company runs a residential cleaning service or a search engine optimization firm. All you want is a meeting.

Research

The first step to improving your odds of success with a cold call is to zero in on the true prospects on your list. Make sure the people you're calling are potential buyers for what you're selling. For example, if you're trying to find potential mortgage-refinancing candidates, you'll want to verify that the people you're calling own their own homes. Or if you're trying to reach human resource managers at companies with more than fifty employees, it may be worth your time to check out each company online to confirm their number of employees.

Useful resources to learn about individuals include the following:

- Search engines like Google and Yahoo!
- Magazine databases available through your library
- Newspaper articles accessed through an online archive
- Biography databases or print directories

Resources for company or business executive information include the following:

- The company's corporate Web site
- Search engines
- Hoovers.com
- Lexis-Nexis
- Magazine databases
- Trade association Web sites
- Competitors' Web sites

Yes, it's an extra step. But unless the company or person who compiled your cold call list can guarantee that each person is a serious prospect, you want to do some digging on your own to save time and come across as more knowledgeable when you make your call.

As you're double-checking your list, make note of useful information you find in your research. Using the example of wanting to contact human resource managers for companies with at least fifty employees, as you're checking into the size of each of your target companies, take a minute to make note of facts about the

---

 Watch Out!

Although it's common courtesy to ask "Is this a good time to talk?" when calling colleagues or clients, it's not a good idea to ask the same question of prospects you are cold calling. The reason? Many will immediately tell you that it's not in order to end the call. After you have a prospect on the phone, don't ask permission, just give it your best shot.

business related to your call. For example, if you aim to convince the HR managers to use your new online help-wanted Web site, it would help your credibility to know the following:

- How many jobs are currently available at the company
- How many jobs the company typically posts in a month at other sites
- An estimate of how much the company is spending at other sites
- Whether there is a particular expertise the company is having trouble finding

With this background information in hand, you're in a much stronger position to catch the attention of the person you are calling—and this is your first challenge when cold calling—and to entice him or her to engage in conversation, rather than ending the call. Having done your homework, you can immediately mention what you know about the company's situation and how you can meet its needs.

After you have your prospect on the phone, whether you actually get the caller on the phone live or are forced to leave a voice message, use a prepared script to keep your message on track.

Script

Although you certainly don't want to sound scripted when you're speaking with someone by phone, drafting the key points you want to make can help ensure you've done all you can to interest the person in hearing more.

 Bright Idea

Stand up! Whenever you're talking on the phone, and especially when you're cold calling, stand up. Pace the floor, if you want to. Standing gives you confidence and helps your voice sound stronger because you have better air flow to your lungs.

Voicemail

There are six key pieces of information you need to convey in an effective voicemail message to a prospect. Of course, there's no guarantee that you'll get a call back or that your call will be answered the next time you try to reach the person, but at least you'll have communicated the reason for your call and heightened awareness of your company.

The six steps to leaving an effective voicemail message are as follows:

1. **Greet the person you're calling.** "Hello," "Good morning," and "Good afternoon" are excellent ways to start off your message.

2. **State who you are and who you represent.** "This is Jeff Smith from Office Copier Corporation calling," is one way to accomplish this.

3. **Explain why you called.** "Our company has just been named the first authorized SuperCopy representative in your area and I'd like to stop by to give you a proposal for handling all of your company's office copy needs." Or "We're running a special offer for customers like you this Saturday. We'll make up to 100 color copies totally free for you on Saturday between 9:00 and 6:00."

4. **Be clear about the benefit to the person you've called.** Examples include a proposal that may save the company money or receiving free copies.

5. **Tell your prospect what you would like him or her to do.** This may range from agreeing to an appointment with you at a particular time, coming in to the store on a certain day, or doing some other activity, such as visiting a Web site or completing a survey.

6. **Thank your prospect and say goodbye.**

At first, such a systematic process may seem stilted or uncomfortable for you, but practice makes perfect and enables you to deliver your message confidently, without sounding rehearsed.

If the individual does not respond to repeated attempts to reach him or her, you may want to try calling before or after normal business hours—assuming this is a business-to-business call. Early in the business day and around the dinner hour are times when some businesspeople are still in the office, without gatekeepers like assistants or secretaries to get in the way.

When consumers don't return calls, you can assume either that they have no interest in your product or service, or that they don't yet have all the information they need to make an informed decision. If the latter is the case, you can try following up with printed material in support of your offerings. But over time, if you get no return call, it would make more sense to cross the person off your prospect list than to continue investing time in calling—unless you're positive the person is a solid prospect.

Live discussion

Voicemail is great because you can leave your carefully crafted message for your prospect without having the person interrupt your flow or cut you off. The downside, of course, is that you don't have the chance to interact with the person receiving the message—it's only one-way communication, and you need two-way communication in order to land an appointment or get a commitment to action from your prospect. You need to have a live discussion with your prospect.

When you reach a live person, use the voicemail script in the preceding section as a guide to opening your discussion. Although there will likely be a back-and-forth discussion between you and your target customer, stay focused on achieving your primary objective, which is to set up an appointment, determine whether he or she has a need for your services, or invite the individual to lunch. The conversation may not be long, and will, with any luck, end with your getting what you ask for.

Bright Idea

Review your research notes in search of some tidbit you have in common with the person you're calling. Did you attend the same college? once work for the same company? have a son in Little League? Bring that into the conversation early to try to form a bond with your prospect based on your similarities.

If you routinely encounter a receptionist or assistant when you call, try to win his or her support or sympathy for your efforts to reach the boss. That person is all that's standing between you and a discussion with your prospect, so do all you can to earn his or her trust and support rather than garnering a reputation as a nuisance.

During a live conversation with someone, you're likely to spend most of your time overcoming his objections to your request for an appointment, or the chance to win his business. To avoid being stopped cold by a "No, we don't use those types of services," or "No, I'm not interested," you'll want to ask questions, rather than immediately start offering product benefits.

To respond to a response that the company doesn't use your type of services, find out why. Does it use something similar? Has the company not had a need? Is the company at all worried about the consequences?

To the "I'm not interested" response, try a similar tact—offer information about your product's or service's primary benefit, and then immediately start asking questions.

Perhaps there isn't a fit between your company and the one you're targeting, or between your offerings and the individual's current needs—and you should admit this to the person you're speaking with. But with a few pointed questions, you can still get a better idea of your prospect's situation. Even when there isn't a current need for what you're selling, you may be able to spot a future scenario in which there will be, such as the purchase of a first home or finalization of a company's budget. Ask for permission to check back, to stay in touch.

Remember one more important point: Don't call more than once a day—at most!—or you'll be branded a pest.

Warm calling

If cold calling involves picking up the phone and dialing someone out of the blue, with whom you have no connection, *warm calling* is reaching out to someone with whom you've had some kind of contact. Warm calling is much easier to do than cold calling because you generally have better odds of getting through and having a live conversation—but that's not guaranteed.

Because of the improved odds of success, some tactics for warming up cold calls include the following:

- Sending marketing literature in advance of a call and indicating when you'll try to reach the recipient, such as "next week" or "on Tuesday"

- Finding a mutual acquaintance and getting an introduction or referral

- Arranging to "bump into" a target prospect, such as at a networking meeting or professional association seminar, and mentioning that you've been meaning to get in touch; then follow up after the meeting with a call

After you're connected to your prospect, you'll want to follow the same type of script you used for your cold calls.

Outsourcing

Instead of using their own employees to telemarket their goods and services via telephone, some companies hand off those activities to telemarketing specialists. In most cases, such telemarketers are charged with making a low-cost sale or setting up an appointment or trial offer for a more expensive service. For example, it may be more cost effective to outsource telemarketing calls to sell magazine subscriptions or to conduct surveys. However, there are some types of calls where outsourcing isn't your best move.

Money Saver

If you're interested in recording an upcoming teleseminar, Great Teleseminars offers a complete package of services—phone lines, recording, and technical support if you need it. Find out more at www.greatteleseminars.com.

If your company's products or services are complex or costly and are typically sold by developing a relationship with your prospect, you're not going to want to hand that relationship-building responsibility over to anyone else. For example, if you're a high-end home remodeler, you're going to want someone on your staff who is knowledgeable and has firsthand experience with such jobs contacting prospective customers to discuss your services. Outsourcing such calls to unqualified people will likely backfire if the person who picks up the phone begins to ask specific questions about the equipment you use, how soon you could start work, or how you've handled a tricky design element in other client homes. Only someone with experience in the business could answer such questions accurately and improve the chances of landing the business.

Telemarketing firms are an excellent resource and can tackle an amazing number of calls in record time, but unless you're willing to thoroughly train them in how to answer specific—and potentially complicated—questions from prospects, I'd suggest you keep that responsibility in house.

Inbound telemarketing

Although telemarketing is generally associated with *outbound* telephone calls, initiated by businesses and received by prospects at home or the office, that's only part of the equation. The other part is encouraging *inbound* calls from prospects. One of the most common ways to do this is to set up a toll-free number if you do business outside of your local area code, so that potential customers can call you at no charge. For customers who do make the call, you'll want to be sure you have trained professionals answering the phone, able to answer the majority of callers' questions.

Another option is to set up a 900-number, which charges callers on a per-minute basis, generally for information or technical support. Because there is a commitment to pay a fee for the call, 900-numbers aren't as much a part of marketing as they are of completing a sale. Today, you'll find them used by computer and software manufacturers as a means of handling technical support questions and by consultants with advice to give.

Teleseminars

One of the more recent applications of telecommunications technology is the teleseminar, which can be a marketing tool or a service in and of itself. Essentially, it's a seminar by phone, as the name suggests. Companies use them to provide information about their products and services and to conduct how-to workshops and discussions. Some businesses charge customers for their participation, while others host teleseminars as part of their marketing toolkit, giving listeners a sample of the expertise and/or services they would enjoy as a customer.

Teleseminars are set up much like a conference call. You contract with a teleseminar company to provide a bridge line into which people can call. Specifically, you reserve a particular call-in number for a timeslot of an hour or two, or more if you need it, and are given a maximum number of callers who can dial in, such as 25, 50, or 200. You are charged for the rental of the line for the time that you use it, and callers pay their own long distance charges to make the call. It's a low-cost way to

 Bright Idea

For help in finding potential telemarketing suppliers, check out the Community button on the American Teleservices Association Web site (www.ataconnect.org), where potential suppliers are listed.

bring many customers together for a presentation and question-and-answer session afterward.

Some consultants who offer such teleseminars also tape them and sell CDs and tapes of the seminar after the fact, creating a new profit center for their business. Other companies offer a free copy of a recent teleseminar to prospects, using it as a marketing tool.

Some of the most successful business owners report that telemarketing in general, and cold calling in particular, set their companies apart from the competition and give them a solid leg up because few other companies are using this marketing tool. For small businesses with low marketing budgets, cold calling can be a way to make contact with prospects without having to invest in expensive materials or advertisements. But as many people have pointed out, it's a numbers game that you have to stick with in order to win.

Just the facts

- Any business that calls consumers in the hopes of selling something—whether it's cheap wireless service or the fruit of the month club—must abide by the Telephone Service Rules (TSR), which includes referencing the Do Not Call Registry, which the FCC developed in 2003, or risk fines of $11,000 per call.

- Businesses calling other businesses are exempt from TSRs unless they are selling nondurable office or cleaning supplies, in which case they must follow them.

- Successful telemarketing efforts typically involve cold calling, and plenty of it. To overcome fear of such calls, research each call beforehand to learn about the consumer's or business's need for your offerings, draft a script to follow, and decide what you want to achieve as a result of your call, such as agreement to review your materials, for example.

- There is a direct relationship between the number of cold calls you make, the number of appointments you secure, and the number of sales you ultimately earn. The more you call, the closer you are to a sale.

- For even better results from your calling, try warming up your prospective customer before you dial their number. Connecting with a potential customer before you call increases the odds that the person will take your call and seriously consider your offerings. Such calls are called warm calls.

- Although telemarketing has generally been viewed as an outbound activity—with callers trying to reach potential customers—recent efforts designed to increase inbound calls, such as teleseminars, are seeing impressive results.

Higher-Cost (But Highly Effective) Marketing Tools

PART V

GET THE SCOOP ON...
Understanding branding basics ▪ Knowing how
your image makes or breaks you ▪ Learning why
consistency is key ▪ Seeing how intangibles
translate into sales

Branding

Branding has become *the* buzzword within the marketing community in the last few years, with companies of all sizes paying much more attention to their image and reputation. Sure, there are plenty of marketing techniques that help generate business in the short-term, such as special promotions, advertising, and cold calling, but *branding*—also called *image building*—is for the long-haul. It involves creating a look and feel that sparks a particular reaction from customers. Marketing methods associated with brand building help support your overall marketing message and create a positive impression that can make the different between getting a customer's business and not.

Most of these methods are intangible, however, and hard to directly link to a particular sale or new customer. Take a store's décor, for example, or employee certification, signage, sponsorships, giveaways, or awards. On their own, each method is unlikely to immediately drive a potential customer to do business with you, but when added to the list of other marketing tools you use, they are like the icing on the cake.

A *brand* is the customers' perception of a particular company or product, which is shaped by their experiences with the company as well as external factors, such as marketing activities, what others say about the business, and what their gut tells them. As other experts have said, it's a combination of what their heads know about the company or product and what their hearts feel. It's the cachet, aura, or feeling about a product—the intangibles that give consumers a warm fuzzy feeling.

What their heads know is based on their experiences, as well as what they've read, heard, smelled—you name it—about the brand. The customer's head processes the tangible, frequently logical, information about the brand, which leads it to a conclusion about doing business with the company.

On the other hand, what their hearts feel and sense about a company may have nothing to do with what their heads know. The heart is purely emotional, and if it decides that your brand is not what it wants or needs, no marketing method is going to get past that short-term and the customer will go elsewhere. On the other hand, if the heart decides that your brand is a must-have, no logic in the world will dissuade customers from spending, or perhaps wasting, their money.

What you can do to win both your customers' heads and hearts is to consistently provide positive experiences, and to back that up with intangible, feel-good marketing activities.

Consistency

At the core of branding is building a positive image of your company and its products or services. And you must do this consistently. A positive image and reputation is possible only when you surround customers with a message and experience that is consistently positive. That is, every marketing method must have a similar look and feel, use similar language, and appear in venues that are consistent with what customers have come to expect.

When that happens, a customer's positive impression of your company is confirmed, and the brand image made stronger.

However, when a marketing program is inconsistent, customers become confused. They wonder which marketing image really represents the company. They lose trust. And you lose their business.

This can happen, for example, when you decide to switch suppliers to your restaurant, and the quality of the food suffers. Your customers start to whisper to each other that, "The food *used* to be so good here." And next time they eat out, they try that new place down the street. Your brand image has been tarnished.

Or suppose your boutique consulting firm places an amateurish-looking ad in a well-respected business publication. Your clients expect to see your firm mentioned in the magazine, but the ad is so poor that they begin to wonder if your firm really knows what it's doing after all. If you're experts, then why would you think that ad was any good, they wonder.

As you're building a brand image, it is critical that each element of your marketing program builds on the last. That when placed next to each other, it would be obvious all the marketing examples came from the same company. If the look, feel, and level of quality exhibited are not consistent, one of your first branding challenges is to unify their appearance. If you can't afford to do it well, then don't do it at all, or you'll risk damaging your reputation.

Awards

Everyone likes to be associated with a winner. All other things being equal, buyers will probably select a recent award-winner over a firm that has not won an award. Why? Because awards signify that a third party has assessed some aspect of your company's work and deemed it top quality.

So how do you win awards? You need to apply for them. Some awards programs request nominations from clients, colleagues, or friends, but most awards competitions allow the companies themselves to recommend that they be considered. There's no shame in thinking that your company rocks.

You may also be surprised at the number and variety of awards programs available, which is why it's a smart idea to evaluate what kinds of awards are going to do the most good for your business. Additionally, because many awards require some type of entry fee, applying for several awards can become costly.

Take a look at which awards programs are a good fit for your company, based on the level of prestige and familiarity with your target audience. Consider all aspects of your business when brainstorming potential types of awards, including the following:

- **Marketing:** There are many awards for well-designed company Web sites, PR programs, advertisements, articles—you name it.

- **Products:** There are awards and competitions for best new product, best improved product, and so on.

- **Corporate policy:** Some organizations seek out best practices in such areas as ethics or human resource management.

- **Location-specific:** Area organizations, such as your local chamber of commerce, frequently sponsor awards for businesses in their service area.

- **Community involvement:** Most nonprofit organizations and charities bestow a best volunteer award to those who have contributed greatly to their success.

- **Professional/trade involvement:** Local groups frequently honor members who have distinguished themselves in some way.

- **Growth-related:** National business magazines, such as *Inc.*, acknowledge small businesses that have significantly increased sales within the last year.

To create a master list of potential awards programs of interest, take a look through magazines you regularly read, and investigate

Bright Idea

When you do win an award, make sure you send out a press release announcing it to the local community and include mention of it on your Web site and in your newsletter.

organizations to which you belong and educational institutions you may be affiliated with. Or try a Google search using the key word "awards" or "business awards" to get a sense of the wide variety of programs out there. Then get to work applying.

Certifications

Although awards are among the least expensive intangible branding activities, becoming certified in a skill or topic area is another—generally reasonably priced—way to boost your company's visibility and reputation.

If you run a technology-related firm, your company or one or more of your information technology (IT) staff members should explore becoming certified in any of the software packages you use, if such certification is viewed as desirable by customers.

Several years ago, having your company certified as ISO 9000 compliant was all the rage, and was supposed to indicate a higher-quality operation. ISO 9000 certification still exists, but the clamor for more companies to become certified seems to have died down in certain industries. You might want to discuss with your clients whether ISO certification would be a plus in their eyes.

On a smaller scale, if members of your staff are knowledgeable in a particular functional area, you might look into whether there is a certification opportunity that would help position your business as more experienced, more skilled, or more knowledgeable. Mechanics, medical technicians, and Web site designers, for example, have the opportunity to become certified in specific programs or types of equipment. Earning that certification sets them apart from other workers who haven't achieved that goal, which can also set your company apart from other companies whose employees have not yet demonstrated their expertise.

And that's what becoming certified is all about—demonstrating that your company and its workers are knowledgeable and worth the money your customers pay you. It's an intangible that adds to your brand and reputation in a positive way.

Promotional products

In addition to touting your knowledgeable employees, another tactic for enhancing customer perceptions of your company is to give them gifts. Seriously.

> ❝ According to the Promotional Products Association, a recent study found that "76.1 percent of respondents could recall the advertiser's name on a promotional product that they had received in the past 12 months. In addition, 75.4 percent of respondents said they kept their promotional product because it was useful. ❞

Investing in products that remind customers of your company and have them think positively of you is often well worth the cost. Although you can spend tens of thousands of dollars on products with your company logo or name on them (often referred to as promotional products, premiums, or giveaways—see Chapter 7), you don't need to. Starting at a hundred dollars or less, you can find products that help keep your company top of mind. Some of the most popular promotional products include the following:

▪ Sticky-back notes with your company's logo, tag line, and contact information are a great way to give customers something useful, and they also have a built-in mechanism to spread the word about your business every time they use them.

- Pens and pencils with your company name on the side are a very inexpensive but practical way to remind customers of your existence.

- Magnets help customers keep your phone number handy—right on their refrigerators.

- Tote bags are a little more expensive, but a nice giveaway at trade shows, where your company name is displayed for all to see.

- Water bottles are another popular choice, especially during warmer months or if your business is fitness-related.

- Mugs are also popular.

If you'd like to have a product or two to give away at presentations, trade shows, or to potential customers with whom you meet, look in your phone book and find a local promotional products dealer, and then call and request some catalogs of popular products to get an idea of what might be effective for your company. Ask for some ideas from them—what might they suggest for your type of business? Ask colleagues in your business in other parts of the country what types of promotional products have worked well for them. And, by all means, ask your customers what gadgets they love, or could use, or use all the time. Ideally, you want to find a product that isn't too expensive, but that fits with your type of business, and that prospects and customers will appreciate and use.

Make sure the product you choose has some kind of tie to your business, or is generic enough—such as with pens or notepads—that you know everyone will use it, or it won't have a positive impact on your brand.

Packaging

How you package your products or services is another way to reinforce your brand image. If you sell a product, the box it is shipped or sold in can communicate how expensive it is—a generic brown box suggests a low budget, while a box with a glossy coating, color printing, and shrink-wrapped plastic suggests that it's upscale. Packaging is critical for branding.

Although packaging is certainly more expensive with consumer products, like perfume, shampoo, and blenders, than industrial products, like ball bearings, tubing, and fiber optic cable, when such goods arrive in clean, good condition, prepared in such a way that it is easy to identify what the shipment contains, you can bet the customer will think positively about the shipper. Just imagine the alternative: Dirty goods thrown haphazardly into a shipping container or truck, with no identifying marks or paperwork. That's a shipping department's nightmare.

But packaging is more than shipping boxes. Packaging includes all the elements that surround a customer's purchase or experience. In a retail store, the packaging of a purchase includes a shopping bag or gift wrap, for example, while a consulting firm's packaging might include the cover of the client's proposal, bound with wire, set within a courier pack for hand delivery.

How your product or service is packaged for delivery impacts your prospect's or customer's reaction to it. Make sure your company's packaging is consistent with the brand image you're after.

Employee dress and/or uniforms

Just as products and services are packaged, so, too, are you and your employees. How you and your employees present themselves in terms of their physical appearance can affect customer perception of your company.

Although not every employee needs to dress in suit and tie, having a dress code can help ensure that their appearance supports your corporate image, whether it's a certain color for pants and shirt or a company-provided shirt or jacket, perhaps with a logo.

In general, the more contact employees have with prospects and customers, the more control you may want to exert over their wardrobe. It's probably less essential that the behind-the-scenes

Bright Idea

Savvy retailers that sell clothing often give employees a sizeable discount to encourage them to buy and wear items sold at the store. Customers who see employees wearing the clothes may spot an outfit they like or see something they wouldn't have normally considered. It's both a branding expense for the company and a perk for employees that helps increase sales.

employees dress in a certain way, but to uphold your corporate image, you may want to specify that certain employees wear a particular type of clothing.

Signage

You might not normally think of signs as critical marketing tools, but without them, your onsite customers may have difficulty finding you. In some cases, a sign is the first experience potential customers have with you, so you want to be sure it's a good one.

> ❝ . . . signs are the most effective, yet least expensive, form of advertising for the small business. ❞
> —U.S. Small Business Administration

Like your logo, company stationery, marketing literature, and Web site (see Chapter 10), all the signs at your business can either support your brand image or be confusing. And if they're confusing, they're not doing you any good.

Outdoor

Signs outside your business are generally used either for identification or for marketing.

Directional signs aid visitors in finding your location, so you'll want to be sure they are large and visible enough for people to see. Consider how far away customers will be when they might first see your sign, and design it so that it's visible from that distance. Working with a professional sign company is a good idea because they can guide you in selecting the appropriate size background and font size for the text.

Sign companies can also help you with any lighting issues, whether the sign ends up being backlit or using spotlights, for nighttime visibility, as well as in selecting the best material for your intended use.

But be sure your sign makes use of your logo (if it's legible at the size you need), or at least reflects your business's image. You don't want a sign that screams "low-budget" if you're selling upscale, luxury services, for example. All of your signs need to support the brand image you want for your company.

Depending on your planned location for your exterior sign, you may also need other signs to lead customers to your door. For example, you may have a sign at the entrance to your complex, but if there are multiple buildings, you may also need one in front of the building to point customers in your direction.

If you are leasing the space where your business is located, you may be required to follow certain signage guidelines that your landlord has set, such as having your sign created in a certain material, color, or size. However, many landlords will take care of having such signs made for you. In addition, check with your town or city first to learn whether it has its own guidelines you need to follow.

Don't limit your thinking to a fixed location sign in front of the building, however. There are a number of ways you can boost awareness of your company's name with signs, including the following:

- On an awning
- On a wall
- On a roof
- In a window
- On a banner

Bright Idea

If you'd like to advertise your company as you're driving around town but want the flexibility to remove the ad, invest in a magnetized sign—typically your logo and contact information—that you can place on the side of your car. The large magnet holds firm, but can be quickly pulled off after hours. Make sure this is appropriate for your type of business, though.

- On a sandwich-board
- On the side of a car or truck
- On a car license plate
- Silkscreened on rear car windows

Be careful not to go overboard with signage, however. You don't want your business to appear cluttered or desperate.

Indoor

After customers have found their way inside your building, warehouse, store, or facility, there may be additional opportunities to help them find where they need to go using interior signage. Directional signs can subtly reinforce your image, assuming you want to be seen as capable and helpful, by appearing frequently on the walls, in hallway corridors, and on doors.

As long as the signs are professionally prepared—no handwritten signs, please!—and have the same appearance, there are few other branding rules you need to worry about.

To decide where you need any signs, start at your front door and work your way through your facility, pretending to be one of your customers. Where in your offices would a sign be helpful? What types of signs are missing? Do you need to update some employee names on the doors?

Customers will appreciate and think more positively about a company that makes it easy for them to maneuver through hallways without getting lost. Indoor signs don't have to cost a lot, but they can certainly have a positive impact.

Sponsorships

Because sponsorships can be quite costly, I've saved them for last in this chapter. If you're looking for brand-enhancing activities to participate in, however, sponsorships can certainly work. Showing your support for a particular organization has a number of image-building benefits:

- You align your company with the organization you sponsor, thereby earning goodwill.

- You position your organization as successful—you have the money to afford the sponsorship.

- You demonstrate an interest in supporting local community organizations or initiatives, which positions the company as altruistic.

- You build awareness and familiarity within the organization's members and supporters.

And although sponsorship of a particular organization may not have an immediate impact on your bottom line, the added awareness of your company's name and services can only help attract customers.

One of the most important aspects of choosing which organization(s) to sponsor is to determine which initiatives are of interest to your target customers. To get the most bang for your buck, you need to sponsor an activity or program that will be familiar to your prospects. Sponsoring an event that is not within your target audience's consciousness will do less for your image than sponsoring a program that your target audience is fiercely concerned with or in support of.

For example, if your target audience is well-to-do parents in your town, find an organization, group, or activity that such parents are very interested in. Perhaps it's a sports team, such as lacrosse or crew; an academic club, such as Odyssey of the Mind; or an event, such as a book fair or special festival. Putting your company name on a program that your target audience wants and supports can only make them feel more positively toward you and perhaps develop a loyalty toward your company.

On the other hand, with this same example business, sponsoring an organization that has nothing to do with young children would probably be less beneficial from a brand-building and marketing perspective. A senior citizens concert or a beer bash, for example, probably would not be attended by parents of young children, so any goodwill that originated would be less likely to result in sales.

There are certainly organizations in your area looking for sponsors, so consider the following:

- Trade shows
- Festivals
- School trips or events
- Sports teams
- Publications
- Competitions
- Parade participation
- Town or city initiatives
- Nonprofits serving humans and animals

Obviously, this is a small list of what types of sponsorships might be available to you, but it may help you zero in on your audience and the types of organizations or activities they care about.

When negotiating sponsorship agreements, look for additional benefits you can request that won't cost the organization any money, but that can put your company in front of your target audience more frequently. Attending organization events, receiving credit as a sponsor in print or on press materials, and/or including an article about your company in the nonprofit's newsletter, for example, could provide additional value for your sponsorship dollars.

Keep in mind, too, that sponsorships can cost anywhere from a few hundred to many millions of dollars (think NASCAR), so you should decide up front if you want to invest your budget in one or two sponsorships, or if you'd rather spread the wealth over several organizations.

Just the facts

- Building a brand and an image involves both tangible and intangible marketing messages. Branding tools that influence customer opinion, but don't directly impact sales, include awards, certifications, uniforms, premiums, signs, and sponsorships. They *do* help keep your company name in the public eye in a positive way, however.

- Awards are among the least expensive intangible branding tools, earning your company kudos and heightened awareness that will benefit you long after the award is announced.

- Becoming certified, or having some employees certified, in a subject area related to your business can position your business as the expert.

- Promotional products are a relatively inexpensive way to remind prospects and customers of your business.

- The more contact you and your employees have with customers, the more control you should take over their attire.

- Signs, whether outdoor or indoor, are one of the least expensive forms of advertising available.

- A sponsorship can be a great way to make your company more familiar to members of your target audience, but is generally more expensive than other tactics. Be sure the event or organization you sponsor is of interest to your target audience.

GET THE SCOOP ON...
Finding lesser-known places to advertise ▪
Knowing why advertising is an important part of
your marketing mix ▪ Getting tips for getting a
better deal ▪ Discovering design do's and don'ts

Advertising

When most people think of marketing, they think "advertising"—paying for space to promote your company in the media, whether it's print, broadcast, Internet, out-of-home, or more specialized niche opportunities. But marketing and advertising are two different things. *Marketing* encompasses all the different ways you make your audience aware of your business, while *advertising* specifically deals with paying for promotional space.

Although advertising is one of the most expensive marketing methods available, buying promotional space in the newspaper or on a sign being dragged behind an airplane is one of the few ways to ensure your message will be distributed the way you want it to be. Sure, public relations is less expensive, but earning publicity is very hit or miss. And even when you do get publicity, it may not be what you had hoped for—either the article gets key pieces of information wrong, isn't as positive as it could be, or is just too short. Making advertising one part of your marketing program is one way to guarantee that your message will

225

Chapter 16

Money Saver

If newspaper is your preferred media for advertising, check out www.mss-standby.com, which sets up remnant advertising buys. *Remnant advertising* is the leftover space ad reps haven't sold, which you may be able to buy for a fraction of the original price if you can create an ad quickly.

be seen in the media you'd like, whether it's during a particular television program, on the radio at a particular hour of the day, or in a certain section of the morning newspaper. But be ready to open up your wallet if you decide to do this—advertising is expensive and not always worth the investment. In fact, I would go so far as to say that small businesses should not consider advertising until they are on their way to being big businesses.

There are advertising opportunities all around you, and in this section, I've divided them into print, broadcast, out-of-home, indoor, and inserts. What these opportunities have in common is that they provide a means of alerting all or many in your target audience to your business and its products or services.

Print advertising

Print advertising opportunities exist on paper. The advantages of a print ad are that people tend to hold on to paper—sometimes for weeks or months, so the ad has a longer shelf life than, say, a TV ad, which is gone in 30 seconds. Of course, some ads are designed to be long-term references, such as in the phone book, and are expected to be around for a year. Accordingly, you pay a fee every month to the phone book publisher for your company's appearance there. Conversely, a newspaper *classified ad,* which appears in the classified section of the paper and consists of just a few words, has a useful life of only one day, which is why most daily newspapers often sell classified ads in units of three or more days, rather than a single day, in the hopes of catching the eye of someone who may not make a habit of scanning the classifieds every day.

Newspaper

To ensure that local residents see your ad, your daily or weekly local newspaper is one of your best bets. However, you should compare the demographic profile (see Chapter 1) of the newspapers' subscribers to see whether they match up with your company's target audience. For example, younger audiences are less likely than older professionals to read the newspaper. Make sure your ad has a strong chance of being seen by the people you want to do business with. If not, don't spend your marketing dollars there.

However, look beyond your daily newspaper to weekly papers, which are almost always less expensive than daily publications, as well as community publications with names like *PennySaver,* or alternative weeklies that appeal to younger audiences.

In addition to subscription papers, there are also freebies distributed locally that cover area events and announcements, and are heavy on ads. It really doesn't matter whether a newspaper costs money or not—the key question is whether people in your target audience will pick it up and read it.

Magazine

National magazines and newspapers can be a cost-effective way for major corporations to make the public aware of their products and services, but rarely are they affordable for small businesses, nor are they appropriate, especially if your target market is local or regional. A national ad is usually overkill for a small business.

However, most magazines do have regional editions that permit you to advertise solely to your local market, rather than consumers hundreds of miles away. The cost is still high, but certainly more economical than a national campaign. And if you see that the magazine's demographics match up well with the demographics of your target audience, it could be worth the investment.

There are also city and state magazines that are worth looking into if your market is local. *Boston* magazine and *Delaware Today* come to mind as examples of these.

Bright Idea

For a comprehensive list of newsletters, check out the Standard Rate and Data Service (SRDS) guide to newsletters, which also lists ad rates, at most libraries.

As with newspapers, ask your magazine advertising representative about remnant space. You may not get the best location, but you might get a terrific value by agreeing to buy an odd-shaped space that was leftover.

Newsletter

Subscription and complimentary newsletters are another potential advertising venue and are usually less expensive than newspaper or magazine ads, presumably because they frequently have a smaller circulation than other print media. However, fewer ads and a targeted audience can be a winning combination for small businesses trying to build recognition among a specific audience. The key is finding a newsletter with readers who closely match your target audience and designing an ad that speaks clearly to them, to get their attention. (I talk about ad design in the "Design Do's and Don'ts" section.)

Some possible organizations that publish newsletters include

- **Corporations:** Some produce both customer and employee newsletters; there may be more than one of each, too.
- **Nonprofits:** Charitable organizations, churches, civic groups, museums, local athletic clubs, and even grassroots political groups often produce newsletters as a way to stay in touch with their constituents.
- **School districts:** These are perfect for businesses catering to parents of school-age children.
- **Healthcare professionals:** Dentists, doctors, hospitals, and clinics all publish newsletters for their clients.

Money Saver

If advertising in a national magazine would break your budget (and it will for most small businesses), look into doing a direct mailing to a portion of its mailing list. You can almost always rent the magazine's subscriber list, using criteria to zero in on your best prospects. Then mail only to those subscribers.

- **Trade organizations:** Professional societies, unions, and trade groups communicate with members using newsletters.

- **Service organizations:** Examples include the local library or recreation center.

These are just a sampling of the range of organizations and professionals who rely on newsletters to spread word of their work. To find a newsletter that could work for you, think about where your target audience likely does business, lives, and participates in community activities. Then find possible newsletters to advertise in.

Phone book

Advertising in your telephone company's phone book can be costly, and in most cases, is unnecessary. Sure, you want to have a white page listing to help customers find your business by name, but do you really need a business box ad? The answer depends on how likely your target audience is to turn to the phone book to find your type of business. Depending on their age and familiarity with the area, they may simply use directory information or head online to a search engine.

For example, if you're a restaurant, a box ad can turn out to be a frequent source of customers. However, if you're an attorney, it's more likely a prospect will ask friends and colleagues for a referral before simply opening the phone book.

Some companies rely almost exclusively on phone book listings for business, while other firms find that prospects that originate from the phone book are time wasters.

Watch Out!

Although your ad rep may suggest that springing for a color phone book ad will boost results from your ad, it all depends on what the other companies on the two-page spread are using. If they are all going with color ads, sticking with a plain yellow or white background will actually make your ad stand out more than another color box.

Before committing to a large ad, start with a smaller ad to see how it performs, and increase the size the next year if you find it's worth the investment, rather than committing to thousands of dollars that may not yield equivalent sales. Test it against your other marketing methods, too.

Advertorial

For complex products and services, an article may do a much better job of explaining features and benefits than a box advertisement. Some newspapers and magazines are now offering a hybrid ad called an *advertorial*. It looks like an article, but it's a paid promotion, like an ad, and is often identified at the top of the page with words like "Paid Advertisement." The tone and style, however, match the magazine, and the piece is written by a regular reporter or freelancer.

Although having readers know that you paid for the article lessens the credibility of the piece, if it clearly communicates the advantages of buying your company's products or services, the note at the top matters less.

If you feel an article is the best choice for your offerings, ask the newspapers or magazines in which you're considering advertising if they run advertorials.

Classifieds

Another place to advertise—probably one of the least expensive—is in the classified section, which generally runs at the end of newspapers and magazines. The price and the space devoted to classified ads is small, but for some opportunities, it works well. For example, alerting entrepreneurs to the opportunity to buy a franchise in your company, advertising a position open at your company, or announcing the availability of space in your building all work well as classified ads.

Because classifieds are generally smaller ads, here are some recommendations for getting the most out of your ad in this section:

- Focus on the major benefit(s) your company or product or service provides.

- Invest the most time coming up with an attention-grabbing headline that summarizes what makes your business or your offerings better than what everyone else is selling.

- Avoid jargon in favor of commonly used words.

- Mention your target audience by name, such as "stay-at-home moms" or "Honda drivers" or "optometrists" to get their attention.

- Offer a guarantee. Offering a guarantee generally increases sales, because you reduce the risk to the customer, but rarely increases your costs because so few customers actually make a return.

- Use words that generate better responses, such as "free," "money," and "save."

- Write in short, crisp sentences.

- Request an ad on the right-hand side of the page, which is more widely read than the left.

- Pages closer to the front of the publication are also better read than those in the back, but competition to land such spots may be strong.

- Don't worry about length as much as whether you've made your point. Some of the best-performing ads are long, so don't stop before you've really grabbed your audience and convinced them to buy.

Promotional announcements regarding new products and services are not generally found in the classifieds, so I wouldn't recommend placing them there—they just won't be read.

Broadcast

Although print is considered the preferred media for business-to-business, broadcast is believed to be a more effective way to reach consumers. The television is on an average of seven hours and forty minutes per day in American homes, according to Nielsen Media Research in 2000, and Americans listen to an average of three hours of radio per weekday, reports the American Radio News Audience Survey. That's a lot of time spent taking in broadcast information.

Yes, Americans spend more time with broadcast media, presenting plenty of daily advertising opportunities. The following sections give you some ideas to keep in mind as you determine whether broadcast advertising makes sense for your company.

Television

Although television advertising is expensive, it can be very cost-effective at reaching a broad cross section of consumers. In addition to buying time on local television stations, which are usually network affiliates—think ABC, CBS, NBC, and FOX—plus PBS and public access channels, you should also investigate cable channel opportunities, which can cost less and provide a more homogenous audience (that is, people with common interests and backgrounds).

 Bright Idea

Some of the most effective ads today, TV or otherwise, feature real people talking about their satisfaction with a particular product or service. These are *candid on-air testimonials,* and they are even more credible when they feature well-known local personalities.

Money Saver

If you intend to do some advertising, investigate using a *freelance media buyer* to recommend which stations and programs best match your target audience and to help determine how many ads of what length would be best given your budget. They can often find better deals for you that save you money.

Many television stations provide production assistance as part of your ad cost, meaning they will help film your ad, but be very careful of cheap-looking TV ads. Make sure to see samples of ads within your price range first.

Radio

Radio ads are, perhaps, most effective at driving traffic to an upcoming event, such as a weekend blowout sale, or the dinner special at your restaurant tomorrow night, although the lead time can't be too far in the future. *Frequency* is also important, meaning that you'll probably have to buy more ads in order to reach a large enough percentage of your target market to make a difference. But the good news is that you can saturate the market for a week or two and then back off until another promotional event comes up. Underwriting your local Public Broadcasting Station is another option, too.

Compared to TV, radio is less expensive, which is the good news. The bad news is that the listening audience pays attention to it for only a short period of time, such as during the drive to and from work. Unless you catch them during those windows of opportunity, your ad reaches fewer people.

Out-of-home advertising

Another means of grabbing your audience's attention during the daily work commute is to invest in out-of-home advertising, which traditionally has meant billboards. However, I'm using this term a little more generally and include bus and train ads, too.

Billboards

Billboards have been shown to be an excellent way of boosting awareness of your business, by putting your company information in front of thousands of drivers every day, depending on which roadside billboard you use. Billboards are rated based on what percentage of the population sees the board on a typical day and are given a 25, 50, 75, or 100 showing, indicating what percent of the population sees it.

The cost of a billboard is twofold: One part covers the rental of the billboard on a monthly basis, and the other covers the production cost to cover the billboard with your message. There are several types of materials used, from paint to paper to vinyl, and they increase in cost depending on the durability, with vinyl having the greatest potential for reuse.

Billboards are great for new businesses because they can quickly increase consumer familiarity with your company. The downside is they won't generate immediate sales. So it's best to supplement billboard advertising with other promotional methods to make a case for doing business with you.

Other tips for making the most of your outdoor investment are as follows:

- Make sure the boards are well lit, or are in a lighted area, or they will be unreadable at night.

- Unless your budget simply won't allow it, opt for vinyl to be assured the colors will be bold and bright and will last the full month (paints and paper have a better chance of breaking down in bad weather).

- Buy one month at a time, and your ad may stay up beyond that timeframe if the following month isn't sold.

- Let the billboard agency design your ad, which should be part of your rental fee, unless you have a graphic design firm you're happy with.

- Because drivers will be zooming by your ad at top speed, keep your message very short—no more than seven or eight words.

- Triple-check your message and photos before approving the finished product, because you won't be able to change it once it's up.

- Choose a billboard location near your business with a very high showing percentage.

Bus, subway, or train ads

Where billboards are designed for drivers, there are also advertising opportunities for bus and train passengers, as well as for anyone on a bus's typical route.

Rail and bus passengers can be presented with a number of promotional messages each day on their journey to work, including ads on the following:

- **Rail platform posters:** Posters up to several feet tall can line the train or bus waiting area.

- **Dioramas:** These large, backlit displays are often found in high traffic areas within train stations and airports.

- **Platform kiosks:** Smaller billboard style ads can appear above platform waste cans and recycling bins.

- **Station message:** Advertisements can virtually fill a train or bus station, adhering to the floor, lining the walls, or being featured on kiosks and booths.

- **Floor decals:** Large posters can be adhered to the floor.

- **Banners:** Hanging signs can be featured on nearly any wall or exterior surface.

- **Car cards:** Inside the bus or train are poster-size ads.

- **Branded train or bus:** The entire interior of a bus or train can be converted to feature only your company's message and images.

- **Overpass ad:** Drivers traveling under railway trestles can be exposed to ads that run the length of the trestle.

Like billboards, these ads are best for building brand awareness versus increasing demand for a particular product or service, and can be compared based on the typical number of daily riders on each bus or train.

In addition to running ads inside the vehicles, it is now possible to completely wrap the exterior of a bus with a promotional message that can be quite eye catching, such as for an upcoming movie debut. Referred to as *rolling billboards,* such ads work best for very visual types of businesses and should stay away from much text, if any. The picture should be able to tell much of the story—if it can't, this may not be the best choice for your advertising dollars.

Indoor opportunities

Today, advertisements appear almost everywhere, on nearly any surface, providing a multitude of opportunities for you to spread your company's message. Because rental of these spaces is relatively new, the advertising fee may be quite reasonable. Just make sure the location puts you in front of *your* target audience, not just consumers in general.

A kiosk

In many public areas, such as malls and airports, stand-alone *kiosks*—upright wooden or metal advertising units—are available for rent, and they feature your company's message on one or more sides. Like billboards, there is a cost to rent the unit and a cost to design and develop the information to be displayed, which is typically under glass.

Depending on the amount of foot traffic, and the demographics of those wandering the walkways, a kiosk could provide significant exposure to your local audience, or to travelers, in the case of an airport.

Movie theatres

Anyone who has been to the movies in the last couple of years has probably noticed a new form of advertising appearing on the movie screen before the movie previews begin. Most programs blend ads from local companies with trivia questions or other quick movie facts for movie fans to read.

> **66** Sixty-nine percent of consumers combine shopping and movie-going, reports Silver Screen Media, potentially predisposing them to acting on information seen on the movie screen. **99**

Most ads are to build awareness, but some do offer specific deals, such as a free doughnut in exchange for that day's ticket stub, or announce a regular promotion in conjunction with the theatre, such as dinner and a movie for $40.

The key to selecting the best movie screen location has to do with proximity to your business and the demographics of those going to see a particular movie, which you can define for the ad agency selling you the ad.

Grocery stores

Just as moviegoers are a captive audience before the show starts, grocery shoppers are equally captive as they wheel around the store in search of this week's meals. Some chains are getting in on the action by stocking shopping carts with space for an ad on the far wall of the cart. Most ads are for consumer products that shoppers may have forgotten they needed—or may not be aware exist—and feature large photos with minimal text.

This may be an opportunity for you if you run a retail store in the same plaza as a grocery store, and could potentially entice shoppers to stop by after they're done stocking up on paper towels and such. Or you could consider building in your own advertising program on carts or baskets that you use in your own store.

Another opportunity many grocers are now presenting is the chance to run an ad on the back of the grocery store's receipts. Again, this works best for retail stores in the immediate vicinity of the grocery store, but area service providers should test it out as well, such as with a coupon or special offer.

Beyond carts and receipts, other in-store opportunities elsewhere include placemats (some restaurants print up paper placemats with ads sponsored by local merchants); tabletops (again in restaurants, and permanently sealed with glossy lacquer); interior signage, such as at a Laundromat; and in display units featuring information about area landmarks and sightseeing spots.

Inserts

Sometimes the cost to advertise your message in a newspaper or magazine is much higher than the cost to *insert* that same message within the newspaper as a stand-alone page.

However, there is the added cost of producing the material to be inserted, whether it's a card, a single sheet of paper, or a flyer. But if you have a large supply of materials already printed, inserting them in your media of choice may make perfect sense.

In addition to inserts within print media outlets, there are plenty of other insert-type opportunities around. In the following sections, I give you a few to start with, but don't be limited by this short list.

Bill or paycheck stuffers

If you think about materials that companies routinely send out, such as paychecks, invoices, and statements, those are prime opportunities for you to insert your own promotional message at no additional cost to the original sender. In exchange for providing all the materials needed and perhaps paying for the stuffing charge the mailing company charges, you may be able to negotiate with a number of area businesses to allow your advertisement to accompany its regular mailings.

Bright Idea

Consider using photo stamps, produced by Stamps.com (www.stamps.com), for example, to promote your company's latest product or announcement. For a very reasonable fee, any photo can be printed on stamps that you can use to mail letters and packages. Why not make use of the space to advertise your company?

For business-to-business advertising, approach nonprofit organizations, country clubs, and educational institutions about allowing your ad to tag along in their next mailing to members or supporters.

Bag stuffers

Retail outlets, such as bookstores (especially college bookstores), frequently allow offers to be inserted in their bags and handed out to customers with their purchases. Although other retail store promotions might not work in this situation, information about area services, such as banks, gas stations, or restaurants, could be paired nicely with retailers.

If retailers in your area are not currently providing such inserts, approach them about it and offer to pay a reasonable fee to have their cashiers place a flyer in each customer's bag.

Door hangers

Okay, it's not technically an insert, but hanging promotional messages on customer's doors is another way to advertise your company's products and services, especially if they are home-related, such as a maid service or a landscaping company.

Having door hangers printed is relatively inexpensive—it's the labor to hang them door by door that makes it fairly inconvenient. But by going door to door, you can pick and choose which neighborhoods to advertise in, and even the houses you approach—perhaps you want only wooden-sided homes, because you sell vinyl siding, for example.

Online Advertising

There are growing opportunities to advertise your business online, from Google and Yahoo! to banner ads to co-promotions with other businesses, all of which are covered in Chapter 10.

Design Do's and Don'ts

No matter what kind of advertising medium you end up selecting, there are some basics of advertising design that you want to be aware of. Although some of the rules change based on the size of the space, the following general guidelines help ensure your ads are viewed, considered, and remembered by your target audience.

Do's

Some of the techniques for designing an eye-catching ad include the following:

- **Do use plenty of white space.** A cluttered ad, filled with too much information or too many images, will interfere with readability. Fewer people will bother reading the ad, and fewer still will respond to or act on it.

- **Do have your company logo professionally designed if you use one.** An amateurish-looking logo reflects poorly on your company and may suggest that you're willing to scrimp on quality.

- **Do use large images.** Size matters when it comes to photos or illustrations—make them as big as possible, taking up the majority of the space whenever possible.

- **Do let photos bleed off the edge.** When photos are used, *bleeding* them off the page, so there is no border, can make the ad seem larger, but it does cost extra.

- **Do use reverse type as an accent.** *Reverse type*—putting white text within a black box—is eye-catching, but only in small doses. Don't use reverse type throughout an ad, or it will lose all impact.

- **Do carefully track your ads and the results they generate.** Know which ad is performing best, and which is worst, and get rid of the worst one(s) the first chance you get.

- **Do use client testimonials in your ads to help convince new customers to try you out.** It helps if they can mention specifics, such as quantities or improvements they have seen.

Don'ts

And where there are do's, there are always don'ts to follow to ensure that your ad doesn't look sloppy or amateurish.

- **Don't use all caps.** It's more difficult to read words that are written in ALL CAPS, so use the technique sparingly, if at all.

- **Don't use color in your headline, because color has been found to make text more difficult to read.** Black is best for text.

- **Don't use too many different types of fonts, or odd ones** that look goofy or are illegible.

- **Don't use too many superlatives,** such as "amazing" or "absolute best," or you'll risk alienating customers who are skeptical.

- **Don't forget to include information on how to reach you,** such as an address, phone number, Web site URL, and/or hours you're open. Use a call-to-action, such as "Call us for a quote" or "Stop by this weekend," to encourage prospects to take the next step toward doing business with you.

- **Don't make your logo or your company name the dominant element in the ad.** What's more important is the problem your business can solve for your prospects—that's what they want to hear.

Advertising works well when your business sells to a rather broad consumer base or to a business-to-business market. The more focused your market, however, the less cost-effective advertising is and the better other methods may work.

Just the facts

- Advertising involves paying the media to devote space or airtime to your business. There are several types of advertising categories, such as print and broadcast—the major ones—as well as outdoor, indoor, and inserts.

- Print advertising opportunities exist in publications, such as newspapers, magazines, newsletters, event programs, and bulletins.

- Broadcast advertising involves buying time on network or cable television channels or radio stations.

- Outdoor advertising consists of billboards, for example, and ads viewed outside the home. They are especially useful for announcing events or alerting drivers to retail stores or activities.

- Indoor advertising, such as on mall kiosks, printed on restaurant placemats, or emblazoned on a poster inside a facility, can be a fairly inexpensive way to increase awareness of your business.

- If your budget won't allow you to advertise in the major media, look for ways to insert your own preprinted marketing literature for less, such as within publications or through a partnership with other area businesses.

- Because advertising is such a visual tool, be sure that your ads are well-designed—using a professional graphic designer helps. Have a single message or theme, use as few different fonts as appropriate, have a focal point, and use only one or two images.

Finding What Works and Sticking With It

GET THE SCOOP ON...
Marketing decision making ▪ Finding the best fit
▪ Knowing your strengths ▪ Hiring help

PART VI

Choices, Choices

Chapter 17

My hope is that you're excited to have read the preceding chapters and gotten a sense of the wide range of marketing methods that are out there for you to use. But if you're feeling a bit overwhelmed, that's understandable, too. Small businesses with limited marketing budgets can have a hard time choosing which methods make the most sense, because there's often pressure to be sure that every method generates results. Calm yourself with the knowledge that they *all* will give you results—but not all will give you sales.

What's important is making a start. Choose from among the long list of possible tools, make your best guess as to which will be the best use of your money, and then track the results that each gives you. Over time, you'll learn which types of marketing tools are best for your business and which ones are disappointing. But you have to start by making some decisions.

The top tier: Selecting the most important activities

The best approach to selecting marketing tools is to review the long list of possibilities and prepare an initial list of methods you think have a strong likelihood of generating sales, based on past experiences and your personal preferences. That is, don't put activities on your list of marketing tools that involve skills you don't have, or types of work you don't want to do, unless you intend to delegate it to someone else.

For example, if you hate public speaking, there is no reason for you to put it on your list of top marketing tools unless you plan to get some public speaking training and overcome that fear. Or if telemarketing isn't your thing, that's fine, don't put it on your marketing action plan (see Chapter 5) unless you'll be paying someone else to make the calls—and if that's the case, do you expect to get the same level of results? Likewise, if you absolutely dread having to write anything, investigating newspaper column opportunities may not be the best use of your time and energy unless you're going to pay someone else to write them for you— which is perfectly reasonable, just more expensive.

Some of the activities that can be especially nerve wracking for entrepreneurs include the following:

- Public speaking
- Networking with people you don't know
- Telemarketing; making phone call after phone call
- Writing letters, articles, brochures, or Web site copy
- Creating a Web site, if you have little technical expertise
- Interacting with customers face to face

I'll bet there is at least one activity on that list that you'd prefer not to partake in. That's fine. There are plenty of different types of marketing activities, and you'd be much smarter, initially at least, to stick with marketing initiatives you'll enjoy and stay with to completion.

Long-term, however, your marketing program will suffer if you can't find a way to get beyond your discomfort, or get around it, such as by retaining consultants or trainers.

For the first couple of years, when so much of your marketing is presumably going to be handled by you, the owner, stick with what you're good at and what you're comfortable with, and then branch out as your resources increase. For now, choose from the initial list provided here (in order of the coverage in this book):

- **Public relations:** Press releases, press kits, white papers, article submissions, radio and television shows, writing a column or book

- **Networking:** Professional or trade association, nonprofit, barter exchange, advisory board, testimonials and referrals

- **Public speaking:** Talks and speeches, seminars, courses, Webinars

- **Online marketing:** Web site, Weblog, e-zine, podcasting, video brochure, CD brochure

- **Printed pieces:** Stationery, thank-you notes, invitations, flyers, newsletters, case studies, brochures, catalogs, posters, direct mail

- **Sales promotion opportunities:** Sampling, co-operative efforts with other firms, special events, frequent buyer program, coupons, rebates, branded products, money-back guarantee

- **In-person marketing:** Appointments and meetings, presentations, trade shows, sandwich boards, flyers

- **Telemarketing:** Cold calling, 800-number, teleseminar

- **Branding:** Awards won, certifications earned, premiums, uniforms, signs, sponsorships

- **Advertising:** Print, broadcast, Internet, outdoor, on-premise, classifieds, co-op, fax, bag stuffers, door hangers, shopping carts, stamps, movie theatres

However, if your business is up and running and you're already in growth mode, you probably have the resources—human and financial—to tackle anything on the preceding list.

Either way, you'll want to go back to your marketing action plan (discussed in Chapter 5) to revisit your target audience, your budget, and your objectives. Which of these activities will best reach your target audience and persuade them to do business with you, at the lowest cost?

Expanding with additional marketing tools

After preparing a list of your must-have marketing tools for the coming year, you should also develop a list of nice-to-have methods as well. These are activities you may not be able to currently afford or that will work well as a follow-up program to something you'll introduce in the coming months.

For example, you may decide that a rewards program is a must-have, because it is relatively low cost to implement and will build loyalty and sales in the short-term. But perhaps you'd also like to spread the word beyond your initial customer base with advertising in the daily newspaper—an activity that is far too costly to commit to this year. In that case, determine under what situation, or at what cost, committing to advertising would be in your best interest. Would it be smart if you could land an ad for $100 a week? $1,500 a month? Whatever the bottom line price, think it through so that you can keep your eye out for opportunities that may come up unexpectedly, such as a great deal on remnant ads, a super price on direct mail postcard printing, or the chance to submit an article to a key trade magazine you'd like to be in.

Even if the activity isn't on your marketing plan for this year, keep a list of future marketing and promotional ideas just in case you hear about a great price or happen to find some additional funds you can allocate toward a new campaign.

In addition to selecting the marketing methods you'll use this year and in future years, you may want to start identifying resources you can turn to for help in producing your marketing programs. Whether you're a solo practitioner or employer of 50 workers, you may decide that turning over some of the aspects of your marketing program to professionals makes a lot of sense.

When to do it yourself; when to delegate

Unless you have a marketing background, or are particularly skilled at developing creative concepts to represent your company's strengths and weaknesses, my advice is to leave such work to professionals—especially at the outset.

When you're in the process of starting a company, or of creating a brand image for a business, you really need the creative talent of marketing professionals to get it right. It may cost a little more to have a professional logo developed or a brochure designed, but long-term, it will be well worth it because you won't feel the need to continually upgrade it, as is often the case when you create something on your own initially, with plans to redo it in the future. The problem with that approach is that for the first few years of your company's existence, if you insist on drawing a logo yourself or patching together a flyer, you'll have amateurish-looking marketing materials representing you, when that may not be the image you wanted to establish for your business.

 Bright Idea

To find qualified marketing consultants and agencies to assist you with your marketing, don't just flip open the phone book. Instead, find out the names of this year's award winners at competitions sponsored by professional organizations like the Public Relations Society of America or American Institute of Graphic Artists.

A smarter approach is to let professionals handle the first round of creative marketing activities. Then, over time, as you hire additional employees who may have design or marketing talent, you can turn over aspects of your marketing program to them. Evolve into eventually handling your own marketing activities, rather than leading off with a do-it-yourself strategy.

What you can do for yourself is to prepare your list of marketing tools you know you want to create, with some thoughts regarding execution—how it will get done.

Do you need an advertising agency?

Most small businesses do not need to hire a full-service advertising agency to complete their marketing projects—it's overkill and can drain your budget by paying higher fees for added services that you don't need. On the other hand, if you're an established company with a significant marketing budget—say, more than $100,000—you may want to look into what a full-service agency can do for you, because you may need that level of ongoing support, and a smaller agency may not have the resources to deliver what you need in a timely manner.

However, if your budget is a few thousand dollars, or even tens of thousands of dollars, one option is a smaller, boutique agency with lower overhead. You need creative ideas, not daily support, so look for an agency that emphasizes its senior professionals, creative talent, and reasonable pricing.

Another strategy is to use smaller firms with expertise in particular types of marketing, such as direct mail, logo development, telemarketing, Web design, and sales promotion, among others. If you have individual campaigns you're developing, you do have the option to pick and choose creative teams to tackle individual projects.

Also consider looking beyond your city limits to firms in neighboring towns or in your region. Sure, you'll probably want to be able to meet with them at least one time to get the ball rolling, but unless you're investing in a very expensive

Watch Out!

One thing to be aware of is that advertising agencies and creative firms will often give a volume discount of sorts to clients who hand them several projects at one time, rather than just one project. So be prepared to pay a little more for a firm to complete only one task, rather than several.

brand-building campaign, weekly face-to-face meetings won't be necessary, and traveling a little farther may net you some spectacular undiscovered talent.

Can you outsource just the creative?

As you divide all the work that needs to be done to complete the various aspects of your marketing plan, you may wonder if it's possible to hand off part of the work and keep some of it in-house to cut expenses. But unless you have a sizeable marketing department with time on their hands, the short answer is, "don't."

Although you may succeed in cutting back on administrative tasks that the creative firm might have had to deal with, the additional work coordinating who's doing what internally and at the agency will eat up any potential savings in time or money, and it may jeopardize your work being completed on time. Also, the more parties involved in a project, the more difficult it is to identify who is responsible when problems arise. My advice is not to do it—either manage the projects internally (using freelancers, as necessary, for parts of the project), or outsource entire projects to professional marketing agencies.

Using freelancers

A *freelancer* is an independent consultant who specializes in one type of work, such as graphic design, writing, programming, public relations, special events management, and so on. They generally work on their own and bill at rates lower than full-service agencies, which have considerable overhead to contend with. On the other hand, by hiring a freelancer, you are now

Watch Out!

Be careful about asking a competitor for a recommendation to a freelancer based on its advertising program or marketing materials—most won't want you working with the same consultants. And most reputable freelancers and consultants wouldn't agree to work with you if they're already working with another firm in your industry.

responsible for any guidance and direction you give them—you miss out on the middleman's creative genius, which is sometimes the most important ingredient.

The benefit of working with freelancers is that the bill is generally considerably lower than if you hired an ad agency. You may also be surprised to discover that many ad agencies use the same freelancers available to you, but when they work through the agency, their hourly fee is marked up by 15 to 20 percent or more.

Carefully weigh your budget, as well as your confidence in your own creativity and vision, before you elect to pull together a team of freelancers to assist you. Depending on how well you communicate your goals, objectives, strategies, and desired image, your end product—the print ad or the logo, for example—can be inspiring or scary.

Before you hire a freelancer, carefully assess how much background you have in the particular area of marketing he or she will be tackling. If you're confident in your familiarity with the process and your ability to manage independent workers, here are some organizations that can point you to qualified freelancers:

- **American Association of Advertising Agencies:** Larger advertising agencies (www.aaaa.org)

- **American Institute of Graphic Artists:** Graphic designers, Web designers (www.aiga.org)

- **American Society of Journalists and Authors:** Writers, copywriters, Web copywriters (www.asja.org)

- **Direct Mail Association:** Direct mail copywriters, mailing list brokers, mailing list houses, printers (www.the-dma.org)
- **Editorial Freelancers Association:** Editors, proofreaders (www.the-efa.org)
- **International Sign Association:** Sign designers, sign printers (www.signs.org)
- **Public Relations Society of America:** Independent public relations practitioners (www.prsa.org)

If the type of freelancer you're looking for isn't listed here, try a Google search to identify potential candidates in your local area. Call your Chamber of Commerce for a list of members in that business category. You might also call companies who have marketing pieces you admire to find out who worked with them—the companies do not even have to be in your industry, but if they have impressive Web sites or terrific press kits, they should be pleased to tell you who helped them.

Collect information from each potential firm or freelancer and set up introductory meetings with a handful you think may fit your needs. Ask them to show you samples of work they've done for other companies, but especially samples of tools you're planning to use. Spend your time evaluating the freelancer's skills in the areas you intend to hire him or her for—compare apples to apples. Ask to see each freelancer's top three direct mail promotions or top three print ads, for example, so that you can compare how they approached the task and what the end result was. Don't waste much time looking at examples of work they've done if you have no intention of doing something similar, such as funky invitations or newsletters. It really doesn't matter if they did a

---

 Watch Out!

Be very wary of posting a hiring need on freelance Web sites like www.elance. com or www.guru.com, where low price is the draw, rather than assurance of a quality deliverable.

Bright Idea

It's always a good idea to get recommendations from colleagues or people in the business of marketing, which is why you want to ask commercial printers which graphic designers they recommend. Printers deal with designers daily and can point you to those who do great work and are great to work with.

great job on a newsletter if you're looking for a professional to tackle a brochure project.

After you narrow your list and select a firm or an individual to work with, you'll want to schedule an *input session,* which is the first working session where you'll share your plans and vision.

Understanding the importance of a creative brief

During that initial meeting, you may be asked if you have a creative brief for the team to review.

A *creative brief* is like a background piece explaining the why's, how's, what's, when's, and where's of your marketing strategy. It's a one- to five-page document that most marketing agencies want to have in-hand before developing any creative ideas for you to review, to be sure they won't be spinning their wheels. Many agencies prepare one for you to review prior to beginning work, but if you can get some thoughts down on paper in preparation, you can further speed the process.

Although a creative brief is typically used at the outset of a project, the key to any successful marketing project is communication. You need to constantly provide input regarding your needs and wants and give feedback on what your ad agency or freelancer shows you. Of course, you'll want to be constructive and kind as you give such feedback if you have any interest in continuing to work with the firm—insults, put-downs, and overly negative comments do not help the team come closer to giving you what you want and may push them to resign the account if you're too nasty.

Your relationship with any outside creative team, or individual, is a partnership. The better you do at communicating what you're looking for, what you like design-wise, what you don't like, what you'd hate to see in your finished product, or the overall style you're going for, the better the result you'll see. And in most cases, what you'll see is ten times better than what you could have come up with on your own.

Just the facts

- With so many marketing methods to choose from, you'll need to narrow the list of tools to ones you can complete and afford in the next year. Start with the tools that will likely have the largest impact on sales, and then assess your skills and budget.

- In preparing your marketing plan to include the various marketing tools you'll be using, don't initially take on a particular activity if you're personally uncomfortable with it. If you hate public speaking or avoid making telephone calls like the plague, don't have them on your list of critical marketing tasks for the first year. Add them later, as you get training to overcome your fears or have the budget to hire others to tackle them.

- Hiring professional marketers to assist you in creating or updating an image for your company is never more important than at the outset. Most importantly, don't put off hiring a professional graphic designer to ensure that your marketing materials don't look amateurish.

- Never, ever try to design your logo yourself, unless you are a trained graphic designer.

- Depending on the size of your marketing budget, you may find that a small marketing firm or group of freelancers can serve your needs very well, at a fraction of the cost of a full-service ad agency. However, if yours is a million-dollar business, a small firm may not have the resources to give you what you need in a timely manner; a full-service agency may be a better fit.

- Hiring a cadre of freelance specialists to tackle your individual projects can work fine and will likely save you some money, but the amount of time required to manage each project, and coordinate the teams of freelancers, may take more time than you have available. If so, find a small ad agency that can take care of the coordination and production, so you can stay focused on your business.

GET THE SCOOP ON...
Tracking results ▪ Building on your success ▪
Using tools of the trade ▪ Spending wisely ▪
Dumping poor performers

Evaluating What's Working and What's Not

I n a perfect world, all your marketing efforts would come to fruition, bringing you more customers and more business than you've ever seen. The good news is that eventually your marketing program may be able to do that for you, but it generally doesn't at the outset.

The only way you'll reach the point of investing money in marketing and having it come back to you many times over is by carefully monitoring the results you get from each marketing tool, testing different variations to identify which element generates the most sales, and eliminating underperforming activities in order to channel those dollars to more effective marketing tools. In essence, you need to find what works best for your business and pump all your money into those marketing outlets.

But the key is knowing which methods work best. Without a means of tracking results, you can waste a lot of money—and many companies do, so don't feel

257

badly if you don't currently know where most of your business is coming from. But resolve to change that so you can get more sales for your marketing dollars.

Tracking marketing methods

To know which marketing methods are bringing in profitable customers—as opposed to inquiries or browsers—you need to track two elements:

- The marketing methods you're using
- The customers who do business with you based on the particular marketing method you used

Although it sounds easy, making a definitive link between the two can often be very difficult, especially if you have several methods in use, such as public relations, sales promotion, advertising, and telemarketing. Customers may come into contact with your business through all of those methods, so how will you decide which gets credit for generating the sale? the first one? the last one?

In most cases, noting the method that actually triggered the purchase makes the most sense. There could have been a hundred different marketing messages the customer received, but the one that really mattered was the one that got the customer to buy, the last one—that's the one you want to pay close attention to.

Of course, the tough part is collecting all the customer data. To make it easy for employees to note where customers originated—whether they came in to your store because of a coupon you printed in your ad or they called to set up a meeting because of an article they read in the national trade magazine for your business—set up a system for customer tracking.

Using a database management system

Because of the number of names you're likely to be dealing with, I recommend creating a central computer file into which you, or your employees, can quickly note relevant information about a prospect or customer. And after customers have been entered into the system, it's fairly easy to add new information.

It's generally easiest if the file is in a contact management system, such as ACT!, or a database, such as MS Access, but you should be fine with any system that's easy to use and has the capacity to hold thousands of names.

You can either allow any employee to update customer records, or you can limit such updates to one person, a point person who gathers new information on a paper form, for example, and then inputs the new information into the system on a regular basis.

Fields (boxes within the database where you type information) to include in the database are as follows:

- Full customer name
- Address
- Phone number
- E-mail address
- Cellphone number
- Web address (for businesses)
- Date of contact/interaction
- Reason for contact
- Where the customer heard about the company
- Product or service of interest
- Any competitors under consideration
- Amount of purchase
- Notes
- Future follow-up

Although the first set of information should be updated infrequently, as is the case when the customer moves or changes jobs, information about any contact with your company, purchases, and mentions of marketing that the customer saw should be updated as frequently as possible.

Money Saver

If you don't currently use ACT! and would like to try it out, go to www.act.com to sign up for a free thirty-day trial of the software. Be aware that after you start to use it, it may be tough to stop. Fortunately, the software is not expensive to buy, with the retail cost currently at under $200.

Tracking how much contact individual customers or prospects have with your company can help you determine how many marketing messages they need to see before the decision to purchase is made. And knowing what they buy and how often, as grocery store shopper cards do, can alert you when that sales cycle lengthens (indicating that your customer may be buying elsewhere) or help you see upticks in demand for particular categories of products.

The database field indicating how the customer heard of you can either be set up as an open-ended field, where the person entering the data can enter whatever the customer reported, or it can be a drop-down menu, from which the typist can only choose from a finite set of options, which would include all the marketing campaigns you have underway.

For purposes of analysis later, it's certainly easier to have a set list of choices in the system, to cut down on variations in responses. For example, one person entering information could report that a customer saw an ad in the daily newspaper, another person could note the actual newspaper name, while someone else might give the date and that the ad was in a paper, but not indicate which one. Providing a limited number of options can cut down on all those variations of the same marketing campaign.

Going low-tech: Simple, but effective methods

If switching to a computerized contact management program is too big a jump for you to make right now, there are much simpler solutions to aid in marketing tracking.

The first is a simple pad of paper with a list, handwritten if need be, of the various marketing tools you're currently using on the left-hand side of the paper. As you talk to customers or process an order, you can simply indicate with a check mark which tool led to that day's inquiry or purchase. At the end of the day, you have a series of hatch marks by each marketing tool, which you can then save and tally by week or month to see which tool brought in the most customers.

Of course, tying those visits back to sales will be difficult unless you're also taking note of which customers bought what. You'll certainly have a sense of which methods customers are responding to, but it will be tough to evaluate which ones are generating the most profitable sales, or which offerings are benefiting the most from your marketing. For that to occur, you need to have a database that links customer names with purchase amounts and marketing methods.

If you run a retail store, you can place a hatch mark by the marketing method that brought the customer in as you ring them out. Or, if you want to track everyone who comes through the door, you can ask as they come in, "How did you hear of us?" or "Did anything in particular bring you in today?"

If you run a restaurant, your cash register reports at the end of the day will tell you how many customers you had and what they spent, but you may not know whether there was a certain advertisement or incentive that enticed patrons in on that particular day unless you ask and make note of it. You can even ask your wait staff to inquire and to jot the response down next to each customer's order. Offering an incentive to employees, such as twenty-five cents per customer note, may help increase the amount of information you receive, too.

And if you're a consulting or service firm, you can use the same approach—noting how prospects heard of you—on a sheet of paper that is tallied by week and matched up to your corporate client database regularly, much like how sales tracking by sales reps is done.

Of course, this system relies on customers being able to tell how they heard of you, or where they received a special offer. Making it easy for them—and you—to identify the source can help tremendously in accurate marketing tracking.

Developing a coding system

Tracking which marketing tool is the winner and which is the loser is a lot easier than you might think. What's important is assigning each marketing initiative a separate number or code that you'll use in results tracking. The code can be numerical, alphabetical, or a random number; just be sure to keep track of which is which.

After you've generated codes for all your current marketing activities, the following sections share some of the many ways you can put them to use.

Testing your message(s)

Just because you got a terrific response to your direct mail flyer and virtually nothing from your Web site does not necessarily mean that you should reallocate your whole marketing budget to direct mail. In fact, you may discover that your Web site can beat the pants off direct mail, once you tweak it.

One of the most important factors prospects consider when evaluating companies is their marketing message. And if that message does not speak directly to your target audience, your marketing results will be less than stellar. But how do you know if your message is off-target or not? You find out by testing.

Although your inclination may be to jump right in and begin running the same ad all over the place to promote your company, a smarter approach is to test it, even on a small, local level, until you find the message that the largest percentage of prospects responds to. Don't commit to a $15,000 ad until you're sure that placing the ad will net you at least $15,000 in business.

That means designing an ad, direct mail flyer, or promotional e-mail with a particular headline and corresponding offer, and then developing one or two variations to run along-side the first ad for comparison. No, you don't want to run two ads in the same newspaper, but you could run one ad for a week and a new one the next week, and then compare the results.

The trick is changing only one element at a time with each new version—don't change the headline *and* the offer, just the headline initially. Or maybe just the offer. If you change more than one element, you won't know what caused any kind of cor-responding change in results.

Whether you're testing a direct mail flyer, ad, coupon, Web site, or sales letter doesn't matter—test, test, and test some more. Look at the following elements until you find the combination that nets the best response from prospects:

- The headline
- The promotional offer
- The price quoted
- The description of your products or services
- The deadline for response
- The requested means of response
- The use of a customer testimonial
- The existence of a guarantee or trial period

This is by no means a comprehensive list of all the aspects you can change and retest, because you may hear directly from your customers that they'd like to see you mention a par-ticular aspect of your business, or that they'd prefer an offer that includes X, when you hadn't ever considered it. And don't assume that the lowest price will necessarily get you the best response. Sometimes, increasing the price actually generates more interest and sales.

Remain flexible even after your initial testing is done and continue checking your marketing tools regularly to be sure you're getting the best response possible.

Knowing when to stop

In your search for the best possible results from your marketing initiatives, don't lose sight of the fact that sometimes more is less. That is, if something isn't working—your cold-call efforts are falling flat, or the full-page phone book ad just isn't delivering any qualified customers—then stop doing it. Stop wasting your money, and then redirect those funds into more rewarding marketing avenues.

What if your marketing plan calls for at least one public speech per month, and you've done six and have gotten nothing positive out of them? Stop giving speeches until you find an opportunity where you're reasonably sure it will be worth the effort. Then try again.

On the other hand, some marketing activities take time to bear fruit—don't scale back too quickly or you'll lose the benefit of all you've invested thus far. This frequently occurs with public relations activities, where you may spend many months sending out announcements, proposing article topics, and keeping in touch with the media with few rewards. Maybe you had a short little blurb one Tuesday and nothing else, and you're feeling like it's a lost cause. It's not.

So, especially with public relations, which can have incredible far-reaching positive effects, don't quit too soon. Sure, scale back if you're unsure of your approach and perhaps consult a PR professional for advice, but don't stop your public relations activities completely.

Similarly, maybe you've spent thousands to develop a Web site and are frustrated that the orders aren't rolling in. You continue to pay your Web host money each month and are wondering if it's really worth the investment. It is. But a talk with a Web consultant would probably be a good idea, to talk about what else you could be doing to drive traffic to the site or to make your services more prominent. However, shutting down your Web site is not a smart move.

Give any marketing tool at least a few months, and then check to see whether there has been any progress. Marketing rarely delivers immediate results, although the long-term rewards can be fantastic. Stick with it.

Just the facts

- It's rare that every marketing initiative will pay off big, and, sometimes, some won't pay off at all. Sure, there will be duds, just as there will be stars, and your challenge is to be able to distinguish one from the other.

- To be able to measure and compare the results you get from each marketing tool, you need to set up a central tracking system. A database that gathers prospect and customer information, along with details of how they heard about you and what prompted them to finally do business with you, is important for gathering information you won't want to miss. Entering the information into a computer database helps you more easily retain and reference it.

- Linking a particular customer or prospect with a certain marketing method is as easy as introducing a unique tracking code that corresponds to a particular marketing activity, such as a direct mail coupon or paycheck stuffer. The code can be alphanumeric, all numeric, or all alphabetical—it doesn't matter as long as you can match it up with a particular marketing tool.

- If you have employees, it's critical that they understand the importance of this information, how to ask for it from customers, and where to record it. A simple form at their desk or by the checkout register can work fine as long as they know when to use it.

- Even before you start assigning tracking codes, be sure the marketing tool you're using will yield the best results. The only way to know if it's a winner is if you test it, comparing the various elements—such as the headline, the offer, the body copy, and so on—to a version with one change made. Comparing tools head to head, modifying one element during each iteration, will enable you to see the impact that each change can have on your results.

- If you see that a marketing tool isn't working—you've tried to improve it but can't—dump it. There's no reason to throw good money after bad, as the saying goes. Instead, direct the funds to a marketing tool that *is* generating good results.

GET THE SCOOP ON...
Getting more out of your marketing investment ■
Integrating your marketing program ■ Recycling
for even better results ■ Repurposing like the pros

Reuse, Recycle, Repurpose

epetition is the name of the game in marketing. The more times customers see your marketing message, the more familiar they become with your company. The more familiar they become with your company and its offerings, the more likely they are to buy from you. So it makes sense that repeating the same messages is the most efficient way to aid this process. Yet too few businesses stick with the same message or approach—they get bored, or they become impatient and make changes too soon. And they miss out on the sales they were just about to make, if only they had stuck with the same marketing tools they had been using.

To get the best results from your marketing, you want to find what works best and then repeat it, over and over again. Your biggest expense is in designing and creating a new marketing tool, such as an ad or Web site, not in reusing it. So, if you find a particular message or story that works, repeat it in a different marketing format, such as reusing a billboard ad on a direct mail flyer, or placing a magazine article profiling your company as a link on your Web site, an excerpt in your newsletter, and a mention in your latest blog. Find what your customers respond to, and then recycle it in as many different formats as you can for the greatest success.

One-shot deals are a waste

A great deal of time and energy goes into developing an effective advertisement, speech, article, or Web site that speaks to your target audience. Every new marketing tool you create takes hours and hours to perfect. Given how much energy went into creating the marketing tool, it makes sense to get all you can out of it, by reusing it time and time again. The only reason not to reuse something you've developed is if it doesn't work—if the results are disappointing.

Instead of viewing each marketing project or opportunity as a one-shot deal, think of it as a reusable resource. Look for ways you can either reuse it exactly as it is or alter it and use it in a new way.

Reuse and recycle

The key to reusing and recycling a marketing tool is to keep an eye out for ways to apply it in its same form. For example, an ad you created for the local newspaper can be reused, perhaps in a different size, for a private newsletter, on a partner's Web site, or in an awards program.

Set a goal of reusing an individual tool five or ten times, or simply adopt the mindset that creating new marketing tools should be a last resort. Reusing what you have is far more effective in terms of the expense as well as building familiarity with your message.

Finding ways to reuse and recycle

Possible reworkings of different marketing tools might include the following:

- **Articles:** Send a copy to your local newspaper, and they may reuse it or at least mention it; request permission to reprint the article, and then use it or excerpt it for your own corporate newsletter; laminate it and display it in your reception area; frame it and hang the magazine cover on the wall; feature it in the News section of your Web site and/or mention it on your homepage; hand it out at upcoming events and presentations; include it in your corporate press kit.

- **Press release:** After distributing it to the media, enclose your most recent press release in your corporate press kit; post it on your Web site; feature the same information in your corporate newsletter; mention it in your blog.

- **Giveaways:** Although companies most frequently order and distribute giveaway items, called premiums, at events such as trade shows, presentations, and meetings, think more broadly about your opportunities to hand such goodies out, such as by holding an online contest and offering a premium item as the prize, announcing a survey in your company newsletter and tempting readers with the promise of a giveaway to the first 25 respondents, giving them to

 Bright Idea

Asking customers what they like and don't like about your marketing is always a good idea. Survey Monkey, at www.surveymonkey.com, is an online tool that can help gather and analyze data. You can create simple surveys for free and receive up to 100 responses, or pay $19.95 for virtually unlimited survey capacity.

every new customer or to new customers who buy more than a certain amount from you, using them as birthday gifts for customers, and offering them as freebies to non-profits who hold silent auctions or fundraising campaigns.

▪ **Sponsorships:** Investing money to support a local sports club, institution or organization, or event can significantly heighten awareness of your business and endear you to fellow supporters of the organization. But don't change your message because it's a one-time event or limited-time sponsorship period. Instead, reuse ads you've already run, perhaps inserting a specific reference to that event, hand out giveaways you've purchased, pull out speeches you've made for other events and shorten or lengthen them if appropriate for this audience. Don't reinvent the wheel every time a new marketing opportunity arises—stick with what you know works.

▪ **Brochures:** Because the biggest cost of producing brochures is in the design and printing, consider printing extras, and then using them in ways other than mailing to prospects, such as converting the brochure to a pdf file and making it available for download on your Web site, including it in your press kit, distributing it whenever and wherever you make a speech or presentation, handing it out at trade shows, and including it in proposals and new business pitches.

 Watch Out!

You, the business owner, will likely become bored with your ads and marketing materials long before your customers do. Don't rush to update print materials or to overhaul your marketing message every couple of years, unless you've learned that they are not working and have settled on a new approach that customers are responding to. Stick with the same message as long as it provides a substantial return on your investment.

You can certainly come up with your own examples and ideas for other ways to reuse and recycle your current marketing tools, too. Just stay focused on finding a new use for what you already have, rather than starting from scratch to develop something you may not need.

Although these are examples of reusing marketing tools in similar ways, you can get even more value from repurposing your materials—using the same information but transforming it into a new format, and a brand-new tool. See the following section.

Figuring out how much you've saved

Intuitively, people know that reusing something, rather than buying a new one, saves money, but calculating exactly how much is saved when it comes to marketing isn't done often enough. The focus in many companies is on the top line—sales generated—rather than profits, which is where marketing savings can have a big impact.

It's hard to compute the exact amount of savings, but the savings are certainly there. One way to estimate savings is to look at what creating a marketing tool from scratch would have cost, versus what you ended up spending by reusing or repurposing. For example, how long would it have taken you to write a newsletter article from scratch, or what would you have paid a writer to draft it, versus being able to recycle portions of a speech you made last month at the Rotary Club?

You can convert time savings to financial savings by multiplying the number of hours you spent on a project by your equivalent hourly rate—your weekly or monthly salary divided by how many hours you typically work in that period.

The other side of the equation, of course, is the results you achieved with those recycled tools. Did your ads really perform just as well the second or third or tenth time they were used? Did the article-turned-direct-mailer really generate as many leads as previous ones created from scratch? It's difficult to

answer those questions unless you have a system for tracking
leads as they are converted to sales. If you routinely make note
of how a customer heard of you and what pushed them to come
in today, or to make the call to you today, you'll be able to monitor which marketing methods work best and determine when
it's time to retire a well-used tool or message (see Chapter 18).

Repurpose

Martha Stewart is my idol when it comes to repurposing—she is
truly a master. She takes an article from her magazine and uses
it as new material for a book, as well as a segment on her television show, a point of discussion for her column, and on her
radio show. She reuses the same basic concept, or topic, but
converts it to a new format for distribution—an article, a book,
a TV demonstration, a newspaper column, and radio broadcast.
You should do the same.

Some suggestions on repurposing your marketing materials
include the following:

- **Articles:** Convert your existing information, which is currently formatted as an article, into a direct mailer that you
  can send to all of your prospects, or redesign it as a white
  paper or report. (If you didn't write the article and don't
  own the copyright, you'll need to receive permission to
  reuse the piece. Skipping this step could cost thousands
  of dollars in penalties and fines.)

- **Blog entries:** With perhaps a little editing and some design
  assistance, you can transform several blog entries into a
  handy booklet to give away to customers and prospects,
  convert them into bylined articles you offer to newspapers
  and magazines, use them as articles or the beginnings of

articles for your newsletter, use them as talking points for a presentation you've been asked to make, request feedback on them and use responses as material for your Web site, or generate article ideas.

- **TV appearance:** If you've had luck landing a guest spot on a local or national television show, make the most of it by repurposing your appearance. After you request a master copy from the television station, or arrange for the segment to be taped by a service, you now have a demo tape you can use to pursue other TV appearances, as well as creating other marketing vehicles. If you have the tape transcribed, you can edit it to develop an article for your newsletter. Or you can convert the tape to digital format and offer a clip on your Web site for visitors to view. You can also have duplicate tapes made and mailed to prospects, depending on the show and whether your message is relevant.

- **Speech or presentation:** After being asked to make a presentation to a local trade or civic organization, don't just file away your notes—repurpose them. Your presentation, if lengthy enough, could be converted into a classroom or online course, for example, or into an article for dissemination to the media, or for use on your Web site or in your newsletter. Photos of your speaking engagement can also be added to your site to demonstrate your poise and talent.

- **Testimonials:** Whenever you receive an e-mail or letter complimenting you or your company on its good work, ask permission to use the contents in several new ways. If it's on company letterhead, frame it and hang it on the wall. Or use all or a portion of the note as a quote for your newsletter, on your Web site, on a direct mailer, and in a background piece for your press kit. Also ask the sender whether he or she might be willing to be a reference for you with other customers—most people are flattered to be asked.

Before you begin to develop a new marketing tool, consider all the many ways it can be repurposed and reused. The more ways an initiative can be transformed into a new tool, the more valuable it is to your business.

Integrated marketing is the most cost effective

In addition to getting as much use out of each individual marketing tool as possible, look for ways to connect your many marketing methods. For example, listing your Web site URL—its Internet address—on every marketing tool, from stationery to receipts to signs and ads, will encourage people to gather more information about your company there. Or offer a free subscription to your company newsletter to customers who call to request it at a special toll-free number, and who also provide their contact information.

Integrated marketing is about connecting your many marketing tools in such a way that they all support each other and increase the likelihood of converting a prospect into a customer. Today, a corporate Web site is generally at the center of any integrated marketing campaign, with customers being directed to a Web site for more information, to participate in a

---

 Bright Idea

To ensure that your marketing pieces are all coordinated, consider creating a style document to assist any graphic designers, Webmasters, and printers you work with. The style document would clearly state what Pantone Matching System (PMS) colors are to be used, the font all corporate materials should feature, as well as any general guidelines for layout.

special promotion, to download information, or to register for a newsletter subscription, for example. To be integrated and connected, every piece of your marketing program should look like it supports all the other components—like they are all from the same company.

Such a strategy does not support one-of-a-kind promotions or ads; every tool should link back to the Web site or a toll-free number, so that you can track what kind of information has been shared and received.

Getting better results without breaking the bank

Marketing can be expensive. Sure, it's worth it if your efforts generate sales, but wouldn't it be great to double or triple your results without having to pump additional money into your marketing budget? That's what reusing, recycling, and repurposing are all about. And it does work. Just ask Martha.

Just the facts

- New isn't always better when it comes to marketing. Because it takes multiple (as many as eight) impressions of an ad, or promotional information, to register in a potential customer's mind, constantly throwing out new marketing messages actually reduces your odds of a sale. Rather than developing new ads, logos, or articles, spend time brainstorming the many ways you can reuse the marketing materials you've already created.

- After you've found a marketing tool that works, as evidenced by higher response rates to direct mailings or advertising, increased presentation of coupons, blistering traffic to your Web site, or a rising number of referrals or leads, aim to reuse it as many ways as possible.

- Repurposing information is all about converting one marketing tool into a totally new format, such as a series of articles into a book or a testimonial letter into an ad.

People who saw the original incarnation of the information will be reminded of your business and the positive information associated with it—few will remember that it was formerly something else.

- Recycling existing material helps to improve marketing results, because you build on the familiarity customers have with your company, and you save money by not having to start fresh in coming up with new material for your company newsletter or Web site, for example.

- Although reusing marketing materials can improve results, integrating multiple marketing methods so that they link back to a Web site or a toll-free number improves customer tracking, which can also boost sales.

- As you reuse, recycle, and repurpose existing material, keep an eye out for information that you may be able to convert to a product. Service businesses can frequently create information products, such as reports, books, booklets, audiocassettes, or subscription newsletters, for example, and then sell through their corporate Web site and create an entirely new profit center.

Appendices

PART VII

Glossary

advertising   Paying the media to promote your business. Today's advertising opportunities go beyond traditional TV, radio, and print into Internet, movie previews, and on-site promotions, for example.

advertorial   A paid ad that is designed to look like an article.

barter exchange   An organization that facilitates and coordinates bartering among its members, which are businesses. Trade credits earned generally equal dollars and can be spent with any of the exchange's members.

blog   Short for Weblog, which refers to an online personal journal that is available for public perusal.

business-to-business (B2B)   When businesses market their products or services to other businesses, rather than consumers.

business-to-consumer (B2C)   When businesses market their products and services directly to consumers.

campaign   A series of marketing efforts initiated at one time to achieve an objective, such as boosting sales or improving familiarity.

case study   A before-and-after scenario written to illustrate how one company or group benefited from using a particular product or service. Also called a success story.

cold calling   Telephoning business prospects without their prior knowledge or contact with your company.

commodity   A product that is sold in bulk and has little or no point of differentiation. Commodities are generally harder to price above the market rate.

competitive advantage   Your strength; that one thing that makes you different from your competition, and gives customers a reason to choose to do business with you over the others.

competitor intelligence   Information gathered about your competition that helps you improve your own.

co-op advertising   Advertising that is partially subsidized by a major manufacturer or distributor in exchange for featuring its company name, product, or logo prominently in the ad.

customer   An individual, group, or organization that makes a purchase from a company.

demographics   Information about an individual that allows them to be grouped with other individuals based on characteristics such as age, gender, ethnicity, marital status, and education level. In the aggregate, such information helps marketers better understand who is buying, or likely to buy, from them.

domain name   The words or letters in the body of a Web site address, not including the suffix (such as .com, .info, or .net).

Do Not Call list   The list of consumers who have registered not to receive phone calls from telemarketers.

elevator speech   A 25-second (or less) summary of what you do, who buys from you, and how they benefit, which you offer while networking with others. The idea is that your introduction is short enough that you can recite it in between elevator stops.

frequently asked questions (FAQs)   Many consumer Web sites have a page listing FAQs in the hopes of answering the most commonly-asked questions.

guerrilla marketing   A term coined by Jay Conrad Levinson for low-cost, effective marketing tactics that small business owners can use. Many are the same as those used by major corporations, but in a different form or applied differently, so that the cost is a fraction of what larger companies pay.

integrated marketing   The practice of linking each marketing tactic with others, so that they all support and complement each other, making the marketing program, as a whole, more effective.

listserv   An online mailing list that enables groups of computer users to share information and communicate with each other. Listservs generally are formed for people with common interests or professions.

market   A group of potential customers.

market segment   A subset of customers and/or potential customers grouped by common characteristics, such as demographics, product usage, or geography.

marketing   The process of alerting potential and current customers to the existence of your company and the features and benefits of your products and services.

mass marketing   Marketing to all consumers, rather than qualified potential customers or market segments.

networking   The practice of meeting new people in the hopes that they can aid the growth of your business at some point. Networking typically involves attending events in order to come in contact with as many potential customers or referral sources as possible.

newsworthy   Information of interest and relevance to a particular target audience. For example, an announcement of a new, high-tech sewing machine may be newsworthy to a sewing and crafting magazine and audience, but not at all newsworthy to a sports publication and its readers.

pitch letter   A one- or two-page letter sent to an editor proposing an article idea. Different from a press release in that the release contains an announcement.

podcast   An information file available for download and playing on an MP3 player or computer.

point-of-purchase (POP) display   Merchandising and promotional display set up near where products are purchased that brings attention to those products and encourages customers to buy.

positioning   The process of creating a particular image of a product or company so that customers think of it in a certain way. For example, Starbucks positions its coffee as high-end, and McDonald's positions its dollar menu as affordable for everyone.

press kit   A two-pocket folder, typically containing several documents supporting a company's important announcement. In addition to a press release, a press kit may also contain background information, frequently asked questions, executive bios, and photos. The purpose of a press kit is to arm reporters with all the information they need to write an article or make an announcement about the company.

press release   A one- to three-page document created to make a business announcement and sent to the media in the hopes that they will use the information in a future broadcast or issue. Press releases follow a specific format.

price point   Price; also refers to the price range at which items sell.

primary research   Market research conducted first-hand, such as through observation, surveys, and focus groups. Often used to supplement existing, published research.

profitable   A business is profitable when products and services can be sold at a price that more than covers all the costs to produce and sell them. The amount of money earned after all costs are covered is called the profit margin.

ProfNet   An online service owned by PR Newswire that connects public relations firms and journalists and writers for a fee. Small businesses can participate through www.PRLeads.com, which charges a monthly fee in exchange for e-mailing information about stories that reporters are working on. Knowing what reporters are writing provides an opportunity to supply useful information or weigh in with an opinion, both of which result in publicity.

prospect   A qualified potential customer.

psychographic   The personality characteristics of a consumer that indicate more about his or her preferences, lifestyle, and purchase reasons.

public relations   Marketing tactics frequently involving the use of the media to communicate a company's image and product or service details, as well as tools that enable potential customers to gain first-hand experience with the company, such as through special events, newsletters, and sampling.

repurpose   To alter the initial format in which information appears in order to create an entirely new marketing vehicle using the same information. Also applies to information products, such as articles and books.

sampling   Marketing tactic that gives potential customers the opportunity to try a product or service before they commit to buying. Examples include car test drives and in-store cooking displays featuring available food ingredients.

secondary research   Market research technique that relies on existing, published data such as newspaper articles, studies, white papers, forum discussions, and so on.

tagline   A short, catchy sentence that describes what a company does.

Thomas Register   A directory of industrial suppliers.

URL   Short for uniform resource locator, which refers to the Web address where information can be found; a Web site address.

warm call   A telemarketing call made to an individual with whom you have had previous contact.

Webinar   A Web-based seminar.

white paper   A multipage report on an issue, product, service, or technology used to increase awareness and to educate the target audience. Considered a public relations method.

Resource Directory

Organizations

American Marketing Association
www.marketingpower.com
311 South Wacker Drive Suite 5800
    Chicago, IL 60606
Phone: 800-AMA-1150

Direct Marketing Association
www.the-dma.org
1120 Avenue of the Americas
    New York, NY 10036-6700
Phone: 212-768-7277

Promotion Marketing Association
www.pmalink.org
257 Park Avenue, New York, NY 10017
Phone: 212-420-1100

Public Relations Society of America
www.prsa.org
33 Maiden Lane, 11th Floor
    New York, NY 10038-5150
Phone: 212-460-1490

Service Corps of Retired Executives
www.score.org
409 3rd Street, SW 6th Floor Washington, DC
    20024
Phone: 800-634-0245

Small Business Administration
www.sba.gov
SBA Answer Desk
6302 Fairview Road, Suite 300
    Charlotte, NC 28210
Phone: 800-827-5722

Toastmasters
www.toastmasters.org
PO Box 9052, Mission Viejo, CA 92690
Phone: 949-858-8255

Web sites

American Marketing Association: www.marketingpower.com/
    bestpractices5339.php

Edward Lowe Foundation: edwardlowe.org/indexa.htm

Guerrilla Marketing: www.gmarketing.com

Hewlett Packard (free tutorials to create custom marketing
    materials in the Business Templates section of the Small
    Business area): www.hp.com

Ideabook (graphic design ideas): www.ideabook.com/
    freebook.htm

Kauffman Foundation: www.entreworld.com

MarketingProfs: www.marketingprofs.com

MarketingSherpa: www.marketingsherpa.com

Microsoft (small business marketing): www.microsoft.com/
    smallbusiness/resources/marketing/hub.mspx

Small Business Administration (marketing basics): www.
    sba.gov/starting_business/marketing/basics.html

Wall Street Journal Startup Journal: www.startupjournal.com

Further Reading

Books

There are many great marketing guides, but these are some that I find myself reading and re-reading for the great examples and insights. I've listed them according to my personal preference, but they're all excellent reads.

Edwards, Paul and Sarah. *Getting Business to Come to You.* Jeremy Tarcher, 1998.

Levinson, Jay Conrad. *Guerrilla Marketing: Secrets for Making Big Profits from Your Small Business.* Houghton Mifflin, 1998.

Dobkin, Jeffrey. *Uncommon Marketing Techniques: Thousands of Tips, Trick and Techniques in Low Cost Marketing Methods.* Danielle Adams Publishing, 2003.

Davidson, Jeffrey P. *Marketing on a Shoestring: Low-Cost Tips for Marketing Your Products or Services.* John Wiley & Sons, 1994.

Allen, Debbie. *Confessions of Shameless Self-Promoters: Great Marketing Gurus Share Their Innovative, Proven, and Low-Cost Marketing Strategies to Maximize Your Success!* McGraw-Hill, 2005.

Yudkin, Marcia. *Marketing Online: Low-Cost, High-Yield Strategies for Small Businesses & Professionals.* Plume, 1995.

Barletta, Martha. *Marketing to Women*. Kaplan Business, 2006.

Popcorn, Faith. *Clicking: 17 Trends That Drive Your Business—And Your Life*. Collins, 1998.

Magazines

Check out the following magazines:

Black Enterprise: www.blackenterprise.com

Business 2.0: www.business2.com

BusinessWeek's Small Biz: www.businessweek.com

Entrepreneur Magazine: www.entrepreneur.com

Fortune Small Business: www.fortune.com

Inc. Magazine: www.inc.com

Small Business Tax News: www.sbtaxnews.com

Newspapers

Newspapers give you a handle on market trends. Try these:

The New York Times: www.nyt.com

USA Today: www.usatoday.com

Wall Street Journal: www.wsj.com

Index

Numerics